Stories That Move

My Life in Many Allegories

Bill Berry

Bill Berry

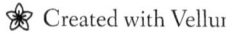

The author would like to thank

```
L O T C W Q R E T X E D D W C F T B R I A N R
N Y I S I H A L L R E C A R L D H Q N T J E U
O M P D N T U Z L E I W K C V O E B A O S Y Z
A A A N S W P F U S N A A F J D E T M O H R W
H U U E T A I R A S A E N T R G P V I R E R K
A U L I O I H A P N H V Y B T E H G A W R E R
N Z K R N N C N A I P I T I F S O T G Q R B E
D Z T F H Y V K J Z E H L T R H T T N G I T F
R T U V F E L I P E T S A T Y T O A I L Z O I
E T K I P E N N W R S K W Y I A N M R O D O N
W O I E U S L I V E D E R A D E I A E R K R N
O C D Z L A U R A S I R H C U R N H D A A D E
X S A N N A E D S T E V E T S B J T A C T M J
P B I L L B O R V M O L D O V A A R D D J O H
Q E O J U G G L E S B O J C K W V A P E E M Q
D J M O L L E S L N N O O D L E S M R I C K U
```

Words are hidden ↑ ↓ → ← and ↘

Contents

Introduction

I've wanted to publish a book for a long time, so I contacted several publishers hoping to sell them on one of my projects. But they each said the same thing: "Your first book should be an entertainment memoir." Their reasoning was sound, and I understood where they were coming from. So why aren't you holding my entertainment memoir in your hand?

Most people know me as the sword swallowing juggler and the taller half of the performance duo, "Rootberry." We successfully performed at colleges, on cruise ships, and at corporate events for over two decades and have met countless people along the way.

Writing that book would be my rags-to-riches story. And at the same time, anyone who's ever had a big dream they've wanted to accomplish can relate to it. But there was one problem; I didn't feel ready to write that book. It felt too big, too fresh. And I still needed to grow as a writer.

But the call to write had never been louder, and the desire to share my words had started to consume my life's purpose. While I struggled with these diverging mindsets, something was brought to my memory as I sat in my favorite chair at Black Crow Coffee in St.

Petersburg, Florida. I love writing short stories and had already been trickling them out on social media for some time and received great feedback. That day, I asked myself a question that changed everything. "What if I set a goal to make 100 short stories that were editor ready? At worst, I'd get some of them off my clipboard and grow as a writer. At best, some of them could be dropped into future manuscripts to make those projects feel a little more attainable."

So, I worked on that for the next year. Some weeks I'd produce three or four stories, others I'd get stuck or busy and produce none. More than once, I'd identify a story I wanted to develop, only to realize I wasn't good enough to write it yet. The rape in Jamaica story, in particular, plagued me. The volume of information and number of characters in that story forced me to set it aside no less than five times before I finally cracked it. But I persevered, and one day while sitting back in that same chair at Black Crow Coffee, the chair I'm sitting in right now as I write this introduction, I counted up the stories I had accumulated. Ninety-three! Excitedly, I messaged my friend, Amy Kochek to tell her the news. "That's awesome," she said. "I love that! So, when are you going to publish your book?"

Ugh! I looked over the stories I'd worked on, and I was only a handful closer to the entertainment memoir the publishers had all asked for. My initial excitement deflated, and I lost the momentum for reaching the original goal of 100 stories. Scrolling to the beginning of the document, I began to re-read/edit all of the stories, tightening and clarifying as I went. Over the next few weeks, the "Stories That Move" idea emerged. Arguably, this should be my third or even fourth book instead of my first. It would probably make the most sense. But I've never gone out of my way to make things easier on myself. It's the motto of jugglers: "There must be a harder way to do this." Anytime we learn something, we then have to make it harder in some way. Why should the journey into authorship be any different?

Move is a word with many meanings. We can be moved in our emotions, thoughts, beliefs, understanding of truth, or our actual physical being. And in some way, all of those meanings could apply to the stories within this book. But move, in the sense of change, might best describe this collection as a whole. These are the experiences that allowed me to discard old ideas that failed to serve, in favor of new ones that better did. But there was one additional criterion I held dear throughout. I wanted the things I recorded to have some universal appeal. If the story had meaning for me and my journey alone, and I couldn't see a message or moral that might benefit others, then it was excluded. I wanted to capture the things that might help others avoid, or better understand the things we face in figuring out who we are.

Some of the stories changed the way I thought about the world, people, religion, or life. Some will be humorous, others tragic. A full life receives a measure of good and bad at different intensities. This compilation is my effort to find meaning in both.

As I collected these moments, I wanted to ensure the utmost accuracy and detail. As often as possible they were recorded within minutes or hours of their occurrence. I've tried to recount the experiences in the way they happened. Non-fiction stories don't always end the way we expect. Still, there's nothing so wonderful as true stories. Looking into the lives of others never fails to give us new perspectives on our own. I hope that when you look through this window, a few things in your own life will become ever so slightly clearer.

These 66 short stories were pared down from a list of 93. Because these most fit the theme of, "Stories That Move," each of them stands alone and could be read individually, though the reader who starts at chapter one and ends with the last chapter will take away a slightly clearer picture than a reader who skips around. Whichever you choose, there will be value in the undertaking.

May this book be our first, but not last time together. Now, let's journey to a bombed-out building in Bosnia, the pantry closet of my childhood home, and explore the subtle probing of the bully. This is, "Stories That Move."

Chapter 1

It's Good to be Alive

Me: "How are you?"

Stranger: "Best day of my life!"

Me: "That's awesome! Why today?"

Stranger: "Every day is the best day of my life. I'm alive."

Me: "That's an amazing way to live."

Then the doors opened, and he stepped off the elevator. As he walked away, I saw a huge scar running down the back of his head and neck until it disappeared down his shirt.

He's right. Today is a good day to be alive.

Chapter 2

Hoover Dam

Several memories vie for the title of, "my oldest memory," but this one perhaps stands out the most. I was young at the time, so of course, I hadn't learned about time and dates yet. I wouldn't learn about them until the second grade. But I do know this memory was long before that. I was probably around two years old when our family went to visit the Hoover Dam.

I don't have any recollection of the drive. The movie in my mind began to play after we arrived. My parents parked our faded brown station wagon at one of the pull-outs beside the road. Then, we all got out to explore. There were a handful of other visitors there, taking pictures and marveling at the 726 ft. drop to the canyon below. I walked to the railing with my two older brothers, and we looked down. It was so far that I couldn't fully comprehend it. I'd looked up at the sky before and thought it big, blue, and seemingly endless. But the sky was just up there, out of the way and bothering no one. This was something different. It was nearly as big as the sky but with a bottom. Instinctually, I sensed danger and something I'd never experienced before entered my body. It was fear. And just as the understanding of my own mortality was born in my brain, I felt a lightness in my feet and pressure under my arms.

Before I even fully realized what was happening, I was carried upward. The railing passed under my feet. I looked down in shock as I saw the now unobstructed void and the faraway river, so tiny in the distance. My oldest brother, probably 12 at the time, was dangling me over the edge, no doubt thinking it was great fun, if only for him. A wail of terror exploded out of me as I tried to struggle for safety but was helpless in his grasp. Panic took me over, but the voice of my thoughts said, "If I struggle too much, he's more likely to drop me." Knowing I was right, I bit back the fright, straitjacketing the feelings in order to stay calm. Alerted by the commotion, my mom ran toward us, screaming for him to stop. He pulled me back to the safe side of the rail. I vaguely remember her snatching me away from him, and him getting in trouble. I do remember that he shrugged it off and accused me of acting up over nothing. It was my first exposure to his psychological terrorism, a penchant he'd refine in the coming years.

And that's all I remember of Hoover Dam, but I can clearly watch this entire scene in my mind 40+ years later. I've since learned this is similar to what some war vets and trauma survivors experience during PTSD related flashbacks. They re-live the moment, just as I re-live this moment.

Despite being unwillingly transformed into wet laundry, and momentarily hung out to dry, there's one thing for which I am endlessly grateful. Ever since that day, many more of my memories have been recorded as movies and stored in a personal vault, providing me with a gift of uncanny, visual recall. True, my ability to stockpile and summon these scenes might have already been there, and maybe this optical way of remembering events would have manifested even without the trauma that day, but I wouldn't change a thing if there was a chance I'd lose this capability. My cinematic memory is a visual library, an interior haven where I can go to experience notable events over and over. Without such a gift, this book might not exist.

Chapter 3

The Blue Box

One day when I was very young, I was playing with army men on the bathroom floor. It was green guys vs. tan guys, and the fighting was fierce. A shampoo bottle from the bathtub was converted into a tower for a sniper to stand on. The roll of toilet paper from the wall lay on its side so a prone rifleman could stealthily wait inside.

Then, having run out of terrain pieces, I opened the cabinet door under the sink to look for anything else I could use to expand the fort. I saw two small blue and white boxes near the back, which I grabbed thinking they'd make great buildings. But as I turned them over, some small torpedo-shaped packages fell on the ground. I picked them up and could feel there was something tubular inside, but I didn't know what. Noticing a zigzag pattern in the packaging, the type they put on things so they're easier to open, I grabbed it with both hands and pulled. Holding up the contents I saw two cardboard tubes, one was slightly bigger than the other, and they were nested one inside the other. There was also a hard piece of cotton packed into one end, while a string hung out the other end. I turned this strange thing every which way hoping to divulge its secrets, but it was a mystery.

Suddenly, while pressing on the smaller tube, the cotton ball shot out of the bigger tube. Ahhh, now it made sense to me. It was a gun of some sort! Sliding the string back through the tubes I tried to reload the cotton ball so I could shoot it again. But the cotton ball expanded, and I couldn't get it back in. I thought, maybe it's like a bazooka and it only shoots once. I opened another one to test my theory, but this one was different. Though it was the same kind of weapon with a string and everything, this one had smooth plastic tubes instead of cardboard ones. And the cotton had a rounded plastic tip protecting it. Pointing it towards a green rifleman nearby I shouted, "Hands up!" When he didn't comply, I pushed hard on the tube with my thumb and blew him away, or at least knocked him over.

This second model was clearly more advanced; its mechanical action smoother. But the little plastic parts that protected the cotton ball grabbed the string preventing it from shooting as far as the other one had. Based on these poor performances, I decided they weren't bazookas. I picked up the box to see if I could figure out what they were for. There were lots of words, but I was too young to read, so I examined the pictures. The simple line drawings showed a series of images; the first, a pair of hands holding the little torpedo; then a simple human butt; then a picture of the tube being pushed into the butt; then the thumb pushing the tube so the cotton ball was left in the butt with the string hanging out; then finally, it showed the tubes being thrown in the trash can. "Huh," I thought, "What a funny device. Why would you need to stop up your butt?"

I didn't have the answer to my question, but since that was clearly what they were for, I figured I should probably try one.

I grabbed another of the blunt-tipped primitive-looking ones. Then taking down my pants I squatted on the floor and slid it in. "That was very uncomfortable," I reflected.

But I still pushed the tube like the drawing said and felt the cotton ball deposit inside. Then, I slid the tube out and threw it in the trashcan by the toilet. Standing, I could feel the string dangling between my butt cheeks, and it kinda tickled. I fancied myself a cat for a moment; a cat with a little string tail.

And that was that, until I realized I wasn't really getting much out of the experience. So, I looked at the box again to see what else I was supposed to do. Farther down the instruction sheet was another set of drawings. This one showed the little hands grabbing the string and removing the cotton ball from the butt. Then they wrapped it in a piece of toilet paper and threw it away. It seemed simple enough, so I squatted down and pulled the string, but it wouldn't budge. I pulled and pulled, but it was really dry, and I couldn't get it to move. Wrapping the string around my finger so I'd have a better grip, I gave it one more solid yank, and it finally started to come out. The removal was even more uncomfortable than the insertion. I started to wonder if this was one of those times when the cure is worse than the disease.

Still, I had only tried the primitive-style torpedo. Maybe the one with the rounded tip worked better. Grabbing one of the fancier ones, I opened it and repeated the process. The contoured tip on this one was significantly smoother, the insertion was almost painless, and even the cotton ball seemed higher quality. It didn't get so dry feeling and was much easier to remove than the first one had been. I decided that should I ever need to use one of these again, I would much prefer the more advanced kind. The difference was so evident that I wondered why they would even make the other ones.

* * *

Around fifth or sixth grade, I finally learned what these torpedoes were for, and I simultaneously knew that telling anyone this story would open me up to teasing of monumental proportions. I imagined the other boys calling me gay for putting something in my butt and the girls being disgusted because I'd used it wrong. I would have tried to defend myself and explain that it wasn't sexual; it was innocent. But those explanations would have been drowned out by the other children pointing and laughing.

Kids are immature. Anything to do with bodies, butts, or periods was gross. So, I never told anyone this story, and it's sat unwritten in the archives of my mind for decades.

But now that it's out, I hope it made you laugh, cringe, or reflect on your silly childhood memories. Innocence is precious; it's where we are open to discovery. Unfortunately, it lasts for such a brief period before judgment overrides our curiosity.

I'd like for this story to be received warmly and for everyone reading it to be mature enough to appreciate its innocent exploration. But I also don't need it to be. The lesson for me is that I don't need to defend these life experiences. Life is funny, it's awkward, it's interesting, and sometimes it isn't experienced in the deemed "typical ways." But who decides what is typical? What is normal?

I wonder, what have you held back about yourself or your experiences for fear of what others might think? How many things are buried in your bones? If something came immediately to mind, I feel for you. I know what it's like to hold those things in. I hope you'll feel ready to share your story one day too.

Chapter 4

Labels

Hearing a strange sound from the pantry, my mother went to investigate. Opening the door, she found one of my brothers, who was about seven at the time, sitting in a large pile of canned food labels. On the shelf next to him sat row after row of denuded cans. He smiled up at her, clearly proud to have unlocked the "delaminate" achievement.

Taking in the scene, and not being one to scold, my mother simply said, "I guess we'll be having mystery meals this month."

He smiled and nodded his head gleefully.

Sending him elsewhere to play, she started cleaning up all the remnants: cream of mushroom, stewed tomatoes, peas in water, creamed corn, refried beans, and many more.

For the next few weeks, whenever my mom would prepare dinner, she'd open one of these "mystery cans." Whatever was inside, that's what we ate.

Campbell's Chicken Noodle soup night wasn't bad. And canned pineapple is edible despite its tinny aftertaste. Peas are peas, so-so at the best of times. But the canned clams were a huge fail! Luckily, Mom didn't make us eat those. Even without a label, asparagus was a champ; nothing else comes in a tall skinny can like that. The short, stubby tuna cans seemed easy to identify until the night a can of cat food snuck into the stack. Mom didn't make us eat that of course, and the cats happily dispatched this extra meal.

It took some time, but eventually we worked our way through all the cans. And despite some unusual food pairings, we got through it.

This story has often come to mind over the last few years.

We're in a loosely similar situation right now as a society. People with the best of intentions peeling off every "label" they can find. While others with similarly good intentions create lists of new ones, aiming to define our ever-expanding beliefs, sexuality, occupations, or gender. And who can say where this exploration will lead us?

What I do know is that "labels" made meal prep much easier. There can be value in knowing what's inside. But I also appreciate that when all the labels had been removed, we experimented with food combinations none of us would have ever considered before. And even if some of those combos failed to change our long-term tastes, refried beans and whirled peas broadened our horizons.

And for that, I am grateful.

I think that as long as we remember that everything on the pantry shelf is perfectly in alignment with someone else's tastes, even if we ourselves don't care for it, in the end, it'll all work out.

Chapter 5

Eating Boogers

One day when I was six years old, my mom had to go somewhere, and instead of taking me along, she let my older brothers babysit me. At some point, my oldest brother looked over his shoulder cautiously to make sure no one would overhear. Then he leaned in closely and said, "Billy, I want to tell you a secret, but you have to promise to never share the secret with anyone."

With serious eyes, I nodded my head and said, "I promise."

Then, he said, "Not even mom; she can't know I taught you this."

I nodded my head again in obedience, "Okay."

He stared at me for a long time, gauging whether or not I could be trusted. But finally, he said, "Okay, if you want to be cool like us, here's what you have to do."

He extended his index finger, then very slowly dug it deep into his nose. He picked in there for a while until he pulled out a big wet booger. And right before my eyes, he put it in his mouth and ate it!

"Ewwwwwwwwwww! Mom said I should never eat my boogers," I shouted.

But here was my oldest brother, my hero, telling me it was the secret to being cool. I had to try! I started to pick my nose just a little bit, then hesitated. "Are you sure?"

Now, my other brother chimed in, "Don't worry Billy, I do it too. It's what all the cool kids do."

Then, he reached into his nose, and he ate a booger, too! Wow, I was convinced! Now, I just had to do it. I reached my finger into my nose. I could feel the warm wet skin, but sure enough, off to the side, I could feel a nice hard booger glued to the inside of my sinus cavity. It was one of those boogers that hold on so tight you worry it might bleed when you break it loose. It was grippy though, like sandpaper, so it wasn't too hard to lever off the wall. Once it separated, it started to slide easily. I realized this would be a good one, hard on one side while wet and mushy on the other. I pulled it out of my nose and brought it up for examination. It was a whopper, at least half an inch long. It was the love child of all my allergies and the result of growing up in a home with four dogs and ten cats. If there was a booger Olympics, this would be a perfect 10. I looked at my brothers, and they both nodded their heads. This was it; I was about to be cool. I went for it, opened my mouth, and put it right in. As soon as I put it in my mouth, my brothers exploded in laughter, literally falling over on the sofa and slamming their hands against the cushions. "I made them happy! They want me to be in their club," I excitedly thought.

I kept going, but the booger was viscous. It wouldn't come off my finger. I really had to scrape at it with my teeth to get it all out from under the nail. But now it was loose, and I could finally enjoy it. I swished it around, thinking "Hum, it's salty, with a slight crunch. Sorta like a super thin Pringles Chip without the potato flavor and wet on one side like the chip had been left in a puddle of water."

I chewed it a few more times, tasting that salty burst with each chomp. Then, without hesitation, I swallowed it. I looked at my brothers, and they had tears of joy streaming down their faces. They both patted me on the back with echoes of praise. "That was great Billy! You can show it to all your friends; just don't show mom."

The next day at school, I did exactly that. I showed a group of my first-grader friends while we were at recess. But when I got to the part where my brothers had slapped me on the back in approval, my friends all gagged and held their hands up, begging me to stop. Word of my newfound "coolness" spread like wildfire and was a blaze that would continue to burn until I changed schools five years later. Between this, my frequent medical absences, and the special ed classes I was required to take because of said absences, I was demoted to the lowest caste of childhood society. Add to that teasing, name-calling, and lonely lunch breaks because no one wanted to sit with the "booger eater."

Despite all of this, that moment with my brothers taught me a great lesson. Sometimes the people you think are on your side don't have your best interests at heart. I wanted my brothers to be the guys I could look up to and be like. But neither of them ever was. They just picked on me, bullied me, and took advantage of my desire for their acceptance.

Eventually, I gave up, and over the years they've each grown dimmer and dimmer in my heart. Today, I have no association with two of them. We are completely estranged. And the other, we perform the customary phone call once a year. I don't know for sure when I stopped loving them, or when I stopped being angry at them, or when I stopped feeling anything at all. And for a long time I felt like it was some terrible failing on my part. Isn't family the one group you love above all? The ones you never turn your back on? Yes, in a perfect world, that is exactly what it's supposed to be. But you don't get to choose your siblings. And for me at least, the ones I got were not individuals who deserved my loyalty. In the beginning, they'd had it. I gave it freely. But there comes a point where you have to say, "I'd rather go it alone than stick fast and be abused."

Chapter 6

The Cootie Girl

I don't know if every elementary school campus has a cootie girl, but ours did. Our cootie girl was named Deanna. She looked like any other kid, nothing in particular stood out about her. But her parents followed some weird religion none of us had ever heard of, and whenever we watched movies at school she always had to leave until it was over. She did her best to fit in, but because of this weird movie thing, everyone shunned her.

I remember one time when we were playing soccer she came up and tried to play too. But neither side wanted her to be on their team. I always played on the underdog team, and to me she was just another underdog, so I walked over and told her she could be on our team. Her face lit up immediately, clearly happy to have the chance to prove herself. Lining up on our side, she took an athletic stance, ready to go. But as soon as the ball was back in play, one of the "cool kids" ran up behind her and deliberately tripped her. She went down hard, and all the kids started laughing and mocking her. She ran off the field in tears. I felt really sorry for her. After that, she tried several times to approach me because I was the only one who was ever kind to her. But I was too afraid of the social pressures to actually be her friend. I wish I'd been strong enough to rise above it and protect her, but I was still small and sickly and afraid of getting beat up myself, so I didn't.

To this day I hate bullies. If all you can do is go along with the crowd and pick on people who can't defend themselves, you're a coward. There's no glory in tripping a scared little girl.

Deanna if you're reading this, I'm sorry I didn't stand up for you.

Chapter 7

First Grade

In first grade, my teacher, Mr. Upton, had a policy that you could not go to the bathroom during class unless you gave up your recess. Well, recess was the only reason I went to school. Recess meant soccer, and I loved soccer. One day, I had to pee so badly, so I asked Mr. Upton to make an exception. But he was adamant, no exceptions; you can go pee, but you lose your recess. Not wanting to miss my recess, I went back and sat down in my chair. Mr. Upton continued teaching his lesson on evaporation. As he spoke, I realized that I had observed water disappearing when it was left out on a hot driveway. In fact, I knew that over time, liquid just disappears.

"That's it," I thought, "I could probably pee right here, and it will all be evaporated before recess!"

Lowering down in my chair, I scooted my butt forward so it hung slightly off the front. Then, I stopped holding it back. Immediately, the pee rushed out and hot liquid filled the right side of my underwear, eventually running down the back of my right leg. My jeans absorbed some of the liquid as I felt the warm wet spreading wider across the backs of my thighs and calves. Once I'd finished, I looked around and was pleased to see that no one had noticed. Then, I sat there quietly, waiting for evaporation to work its magic.

A few minutes later the little girl in front of me shuffled her little black shoes, which made a splashing sound. She leaned over to investigate and seeing the liquid, followed it back to its source – me. Realizing what it was, her eyes grew big. She stood up and walked over to the teacher. He asked her what was the matter, and she cupped her hand over her mouth indicating that she wanted to whisper something in his ear. I couldn't hear but had a pretty good idea what it was because his eyes grew as wide as hers.

The next thing I remember is walking with Mr. Upton to the nurse's office so they could call my mom for a change of clothes. He asked me why I had done it, and I explained that I wasn't willing to give up my recess. I don't remember much more of that incident once I got to the nurse's office, but it's the earliest memory I have of a mindset that has helped me on numerous occasions since. I've never really been afraid to charter a new path or take a unique approach to overcoming obstacles.

As you go through life, there will be things you want to accomplish, but there will also be things blocking you from doing them. Some of those blocks will be flexible, some of those blocks will require sacrifice, and some of those blocks will be completely immobile requiring you to reformulate your entire approach to achieving your goals. But the point is, most blocks are not absolute. Mr. Upton had made a global rule to discourage kids from asking to use the restroom frivolously. You could go, but you would lose your recess and it worked on kids who would've otherwise abused the privilege. But I had never abused the privilege. That was the only time I'd ever asked to go. I even asked him to make an exception, but he refused, choosing to uphold the rules instead of recognizing the exception. So, I took the path most would never have considered, something I've often done since (not the peeing my pants part, the out of the box thinking part). And yes, it created some unusual circumstances, but it also allowed me to live a life far bigger than the one I was offered.

Adventure doesn't live down the paths with handrails. It's where the weeds and the trees grow, it's where the map ends, just past the edge of our comfort zone. That's where I've learned the most about myself. How different life might be if everyone took those paths because those are the paths where dreams live.

Chapter 8

Throwing Rocks

Police Officer: "I hear you were throwing rocks?"

Seven-year-old me: "No."

Police Officer: "Well, your neighbor says you were. She said you threw some at her."

Seven-year-old me: "No!"

Police Officer: "You know that's assault. I can take you to jail for that."

Seven-year-old me: "But I didn't throw anything!"

Police Officer: "Well, you're really lucky because they've decided not to press charges. But if you ever do anything like that again it's gonna be a real bad day for you." His stern eyes told me he was serious as he looked up at my mom who was standing behind me.

"I'm going to file my report, so this incident is on record. You'd best keep a close eye on him." Then he turned and walked back across our lawn towards the neighbor who'd called it in.

I was stunned. No one had ever threatened to take my freedom away before. Especially for something I hadn't even done. But it was my word against theirs, and I realized no one was going to believe a kid if an adult made the accusation. It felt really unfair, and for a long time, I didn't trust the police.

But, like most things, it's not so simple.

When the officer arrived that day, he didn't know the backstory.

He didn't know that the neighbors who called that day terrorized everyone in our neighborhood.

He didn't know that they took us to court over a tree in our yard, or that the judge threw out the case in disgust.

He didn't know they called code enforcement every time the bushes in our front yard were 36" or taller (we saw them out there measuring the height).

He didn't know they kicked our rabbit and didn't see them beat our dog over the head with a stick.

All the police officer knew was that a call came in saying some troublesome kid was throwing rocks at an old lady. So, of course he showed up ready to make an impression. He was trying to scare some kid straight, and he was trying to do his job. I get it, now. There's no way he could have known she was lying.

Still, he was prepared to wield his power on her word alone, and I had lost the battle before it had even begun. Because people don't believe kids; they believe adults.

I wonder how often situations like this happen, just with different variables. It's a fantasy to believe that laws always uphold justice. Sometimes they do of course, and we need them to put away dangerous people. But sometimes the law gets it wrong, and justice is not always served. The law is only as good as its interpretation, and in the fallible hands of human beings, our judgment won't always be perfect.

This experience with the officer that day gave me so much sympathy for police and citizens alike. We live in an imperfect world where a person can do all the "right things" and still get it wrong sometimes.

* * *

Three decades later, I got talking with a retired police officer. A kind hearted soul who told me a story.

One time he'd gotten a report that a man in a black hat and a grey hoodie was waving a gun around a convenience store. They responded to the call. As they approached the scene, an update came over the radio that the man had shot the clerk and taken the cash. As they pulled into the parking lot they saw the man in the black hat and grey hoodie walking towards a car. Pulling into position they jumped out and shouted for him to "freeze". The man in the hoodie kept walking. They shouted again, and again, but he acted like they weren't there at all. Two more police cars pulled in with their sirens blaring, and that got his attention. He turned around to face the officers who continued to shout "Freeze, put your hands up!" But the man in the black hat and grey hoodie didn't freeze, instead he lifted his sweater up and reached into the front of his pants. The officers knew the shopkeeper had just been shot, they knew the suspect was armed and dangerous, and they feared for their lives. So they opened fire.

Tragically, the man had only stopped to use the bathroom. He had no idea a robbery had even taken place. The reason he'd ignored the officers' orders was because he'd had his headphones on, and with the music blaring, he'd been unable to hear their commands. When he finally realized what was happening, he lifted his sweater so he could turn off the music player clipped to his belt. That's when he was shot.

As the officer relayed the tale, his eyes grew glassy with fought-back tears, then he said:

"Technically, we did what we were supposed to do. In the academy we're taught to defend ourselves when someone goes for a gun. And with the information we had, we thought he was the bad guy, but he wasn't. Before that, I'd always thought that there's a right thing and wrong in every situation, but life's not that simple. In reality, there's the right thing at the right time, the right thing at the wrong time, the wrong thing at the right time, and the wrong thing at the wrong time."

Seeing my puzzlement, he continued.

"If the man had actually been the robber going for his gun, our firing on him would have been the right thing at the right time. But he wasn't the perpetrator; it was mistaken identity. So even though our actions were technically correct, even though we did what the text-book taught us, it was the right thing but at the wrong time. If we hadn't opened fire, and then later found out the suspect wasn't the perpetrator after all, it would have technically been the wrong thing for us to do, but it would have been the right time. And if the man had actually been the robber going for a gun and we hadn't opened fire, me or one of the other officers might have been injured or killed, which would have meant holding our fire was the wrong thing to do, and it would have been the wrong time."

We sat in silence for a moment as I tried to process what he'd said.

Then he looked at me one more time and said, "We were eventually cleared of any wrongdoing. But someone's son or husband never came home. And there's nothing I can do that will ever make it better, nothing I can say to make it right. His family probably hates every police officer they see, and I don't blame them. I would too in their position. I tried to do the right things at the right times, but even with the best intentions, sometimes things still go terribly wrong."

Chapter 9

Water Park Wedgie

As I waited in line for the "You must be this tall to ride" sign I thought, "I know I'm tall enough this year!" Last season they made me ride with my mom because I wasn't tall enough to go by myself. I told them I was a good swimmer, but the lifeguard still said no. *Rules.* But this year I knew I'd grown; they'd have to let me ride.

The lifeguard motioned for me to get in position without even checking my height. *Yes!* I set my green and blue tube in the water and climbed in. He held one of the tube's plastic handles and said "Wait for the red light to turn green. Stay in your tube at all times for safety."

I nodded my head in acknowledgment. The light changed, and he let go of the handle. The ride was faster than I remembered, and the tube bounced back and forth as it went through the turns. Every few seconds the journey was punctuated by jarring collisions with the "speed bumps" the water park had added in the off season. Each of them was the size of a water bottle. You could see where they'd cut the blue fabric to slide the bumps under the liner. The ride was fun, but once I was a few turns away from the lifeguard (and less likely to get in trouble), I decided to *fall out accidentally* on the next big turn. As the next turn approached, I pushed hard on the side handle and got the desired effect, the tube flipped over. I *lost* the tube and gleefully continued the ride on my bare back. A moment later, I clipped one of the speedbumps and was surprised by the sharp pain it gave me in my elbow. Then I hit another one and it hurt just as much.

Blessedly I was able to maneuver and avoid the next couple of bumps, but near the end of the slide it got steeper which increased my speed. Chlorinated water splashed into my eyes and I couldn't see where I was going. I hit the next series of speed bumps straight on and one of them grabbed my bathing suit. The suit tightened and ripped straight up giving me a herculean wedgie. The pressure was so intense, it forced my asscheeks apart as it simultaneously injected what felt like a gallon of water directly into my rectum. Mercifully, the bump released my suit, freeing me to endure two more of the jarring bumps before reaching the bottom. Splash landing into the pool at the end, I walked straight legged over to the pool's stairs to exit. It felt like my insides were going to explode. Like I had the world's biggest fart needing to escape. So as soon as I got clear of the pool, I pushed that fart out. The feeling of warm water cascaded down my legs and instantly I realized I was peeing out of my butt. I looked down to see if I'd shat myself, but luckily the water was clear, and no one took any notice of the excess water dripping off of me.

Prior to this book, I have never told this story, but there is a moral here. Sometimes rules that seem silly, like "Stay in your tube at all times for safety," are not there just to ruin your fun. Sometimes the rule makers know something you don't. Sometimes those silly *rules* have a good reason for being there.

Chapter 10

Go Kart

"**D**ad, I want to build a go-cart."

Standing in the driveway in front of our garage, he'd been painting a 4 x 8 sheet of MDO plywood for a field sign job. He ran our family business out of that garage for years, and most nights, he'd be out there working.

Setting his paint roller down, he pointed and said, "You can use anything in the woodpile, you can use any of the hand tools, and there's an old set of roller skate wheels under the bench if you want to use those."

This was not at all what I'd expected; I figured he'd help me build it. But the gauntlet had been thrown down, and I had been given permission to build whatever I wanted. I didn't know the first thing about building go-karts. I didn't have a plan, and I'd never even seen a real go kart up close. The closest I'd ever been was at my friend's house, which was on a hill. We'd take turns sitting in cardboard boxes placed on top of skateboards to race down the hill as fast as we could.

Despite this, when I saw that my dad had returned to his painting, I got to work. First, I pulled out a bunch of wood and prioritized the pieces that looked about the right size to save time on cutting. I grabbed a hammer and some nails. While setting up the chosen wood, I found one that made a good floor. There were two other pieces that looked like they would be good sides. I arranged the wood together and nailed pieces of plywood directly into the side on the base. There was no framing or structure, just plywood to plywood. Another piece went across the back and was nailed into the plywood siding and base. At that point, I was out of plywood that could be used easily without cutting, so I started cutting a piece by hand to go across the front. The old rusty handsaw I'd been assigned was as dull as a butter knife. It took forever, but I managed to cut the final piece of plywood for the front of the cart. Then, I nailed it on.

I'd worked for hours to create a go cart, and it was finally taking shape. I could already imagine myself flying down the street in front of my friend's house. It was going to be great. My dad walked up and asked how things were going, and I proudly showed him what I'd achieved. I was about to ask him about the wheels when he picked up a hammer. With one swift rap, he hit the front of my go kart, knocking the entire front end off. I looked down at the splintered plywood with nails sticking out in every direction, and realizing it was ruined, I started crying. He began to say something, but I was so upset I ran into the house. I cried into my pillow for some time before regaining my composure. "Why would he do that? I worked so hard on that," I thought.

After I dried my tears, I walked back out into the living room and saw him through the window. He was still working in the driveway, painting more sheets of plywood. Eventually, I went back outside and plopped down next to the broken go-kart, sulking over its destruction. When my dad saw me, he set down his paint roller and wandered over to join me. He sat on the concrete next to me, and we both looked at the go-kart. He spoke first, "I didn't mean to upset you, but I had to show you something. What you built was not safe." Pointing to the front end of the go-kart he continued, "See how easily the front end came off? That's where your feet would have gone. And had you been going down the road and the same thing happened, you could have gotten really hurt. I'm your father, and it's my job to protect you. Understand?"

Still angry but understanding, I nodded my head and said, "Yeah."

"Okay, so look here. If you had cut this piece of wood shorter, it would have been sandwiched between these outside boards, and that would have been much stronger. See that?"

I nodded, comprehending the difference his suggestion would have made.

"Also, you had these sheeting pieces but no framing. You need to start with a frame, then attach your sheeting pieces to give the frame rigidity like this."

He demonstrated with a couple of 2x4s and a sheet of plywood, and it all made sense.

"Okay," he said, "Make those changes and we'll see about getting you some wheels."

He stood and went back to his work.

I agreed with everything he'd said, but after all the work I'd done, I didn't have the resolve to do it over again. Every cut with that handsaw was agony, and I would have had to make lots of cuts to get it right. So, I abandoned the project, thinking the whole idea was a failure.

Two weeks later, my dad walked into the house and said, "Hey, you wanna help me?"

"Sure," I said. "What are we doing?"

"We're gonna build a go-kart," he answered.

"Really?!" I was ecstatic.

For the next few hours, we worked in the garage. He showed me how to build a frame, sheet it, and the difference between nails and screws, along with dozens of other little tips and tricks that stuck with me ever since. We disassembled an old hand cart to scavenge its wheels, and I learned how to make a cotter pin (a part that held the wheels in place but still allowed them to spin). We cut up an old pair of roller skates for the rear wheels and used a rope to create a primitive but effective steering system. Still no brakes, but it was the 80's. We didn't need brakes or helmets in the 80's.

At the end of the day, I had the coolest franken-go-kart west of the Mississippi. I couldn't wait to try it out with my friends. But even better than the kart itself was the lesson my father taught me that day.

He let me fail.

And in doing so, I saw why my ideas didn't work. He let me do it wrong so I could better appreciate the ways of doing it right. My dad understood that some lessons are hard, but they shouldn't be avoided. I learned that when you fail, you learn far more than when you succeed. So, fail. Do it quickly, extravagantly, and without fear because there is no faster way to succeed.

Chapter 11

Billy & Goliath

I was six years old, and my mother was out. She had left me in the questionable care of my teenage brother. Unsurprisingly, he had begun to exercise dictatorial power over me, and he was determined to make this a historical night. Little did we know he was going to get that wish.

I didn't understand his aggression that day. Maybe he had begun experimenting with drugs or was dealing with normal adolescent hormones. I'm not sure. But to childhood me, he was just a bully.

I remember him coming across the living room towards me, and knowing that my only chance was to run, I ran! I turned and raced across the kitchen. I could hear him barreling after me. I dashed across the entry hall into the second bathroom, then out the other side of the bathroom into the third bedroom. Then I sprinted out of the third bedroom's secondary door into the master hallway, making a hard 90° turn to the right. I passed into the living room, but I had to be careful here. Our house was a loop and also a figure 8. If he doubled back at the entry hall, he could head me off between the living and dining rooms. I slowed slightly to make sure this wasn't happening, but I heard him in the hall behind me. Run! I flew across the living room, into the dining room, another hard 90° to the right and I was back into the kitchen where I started. But he wasn't giving up!

Back into the entry hallway I went, but I took the figure 8 route myself, hard 90° to the right, and I was back in the living room. I was hopeful that this change of route would catch him by surprise, and it did. He hurried across the hallway and into the second bathroom before he realized he'd passed me. This gave me a few seconds' lead, and I took advantage of it. Positioning myself an equal distance from the second bathroom and the master hallway, I had an escape route no matter which way he came from.

I waited, ready to bolt. But it got really quiet. He stopped yelling and stopped running. What was happening? A few moments later, I saw him walking calmly out of the master hallway, an air of innocence about him. He started speaking softly ::friendship:: ::relax:: ::forgiveness::, he said. But I wasn't buying a word of it. He continued towards me ::trust:: ::loosen up::, I backed away and pressed towards the dining room. He came closer, and I could hear the slight jump in his voice. Under the words meant to win my confidence I sensed the change; he knew he had me. Even though he had only taken a few more steps, with them he'd effectively cut off every escape route except the kitchen. And without a running start, I might not be able to get away that way either. I guesstimated I had a 50/50 chance if I bolted. He kept coming, so the odds dropped to 40/60. I decided to try, but just as I was about to dart across the kitchen, my eyes fell on the dining room table. There were dirty dishes and remnants from yesterday's spaghetti dinner. But that's not what caught my eye. Inches from my hand was a dinner fork. Without knowing why, I picked it up. I felt him hesitate, his brain calculating this new variable. But he continued towards me, still thinking the odds were in his favor. I thought he was right. 30/70. He continued his monologue ::reconciliation:: ::misunderstanding::. I defensively held the sauce-encrusted, four tined weapon, lifting my eyes to meet his. I had decided to face Goliath. Goliath stopped in his tracks, his expression twisting. I watched as the thin veil of reconciliation melted away, replaced by the more familiar anger and belligerence. In a menacing tone he whispered, "Don't you throw that!"

I hadn't planned to throw it. I didn't have a plan at all, but once he said that I had no choice.

The decision was unconscious and reflexive. The fork left my hand. It tumbled end over end as it flew towards him. Before the fork had even reached its destination, I had already turned into the kitchen, hopeful to make my escape. Out of the corner of my eye I saw his right-hand reach forward and down in a defensive gesture. I heard him yell, "No!"

Back through the kitchen I sprinted, out the front door, down the driveway. My bare feet pounded the concrete, but I didn't stop. I didn't look back. I knew in my young brain that being caught would hurt, and I didn't want to hurt. The neighbors' houses whizzed by. I made it to the end of the block, but my mom always said I wasn't allowed to cross the street by myself. So, I veered left. I needed to continue putting distance between us. But as I turned the corner, I could see peripherally that he wasn't giving chase. I allowed myself to slow a bit, then stopped.

Waiting a few minutes to be sure it was safe, I cautiously walked back the way I came. I was on guard. He could jump out from anywhere, but I didn't see any sign of him. Eventually I saw our little yellow house, and all seemed quiet. In our front yard there was a large overgrown Oleander hedgerow separating our yard from the neighbor's. Its leaves rustled lazily in the hot California wind. As quietly as possible, I snuck to the hedge, dropped to my hands and knees, and crawled into the thicket.

There was a small clearing in the middle that I knew well. It was my secret hideaway. With my hands, I cleared away some of the fresh fallen leaves, revealing the earthen floor. A few bugs scrambled for cover, agitated that I'd removed their debris canopy. Sitting cross legged and feeling mostly safe in my haven, I settled in to wait. I had no cell phone, no game system, and no iPod. It would be years before these things were invented. Absentmindedly, I began to bite my fingernails, trying to process everything that had just happened. "Ouch!" I was zapped out of my reverie when one stubborn nail tore too deeply. I evaluated the still attached hangnail that has ripped into the quick. I decided that the best way to fix it was to tear it out quickly. That way, it would only hurt for a second. I placed the offending finger in my mouth and found the nail with my teeth. Biting it tightly, I gave a quick jerk and the nail pulled off in a flash of bright pain. It bled a little, then settled into a comfortable throb, the pain spiking slightly after each heartbeat. I continued until every finger had been serviced. And when I ran out of nails, I started on the cuticles. Time passed.

Once the skin around the nails had become too raw to continue. I was forced to stop but was still bored. I looked down at my bare feet. They were dirty and calloused, but I noticed my toenails were getting a little long. I started picking at them, gently removing the extra length. But a few were adamant about staying put. Because I had chewed my fingernails so short, it was hard to get a good tear in the toenail started. "No problem," I thought and picked up my foot with my hands, bringing it towards my mouth. Starting with the big toe, I typewriter chewed my way across the excess. It was much thicker than a fingernail, so I had to bite hard. Occasionally my teeth cracked into each other when the keratin gave way. Soon enough though, the nail was separated, leaving a satisfyingly flush edge behind. I noted the gritty texture of the toenail as I chewed it. Much dirtier than a fingernail. I kept at it though, and its firm structure began to yield, slowly turning to mush. Once the sharp edges were gone, it was safe to eat. You don't want to try and swallow a big toenail without properly chewing it first. I continued along methodically until all ten toenails had been manicured, then made an assessment. I only had one bleeding finger, so it had been a successful trimming.

More time passed until I finally saw my mom's white 70's model Toyota Corolla station wagon pull into the driveway. I watched as she got out and opened the hatchback. Loading her arms with several bags of groceries, she made her way inside. The cavalry had arrived, and I was safe again. Barely a minute later she rushed back outside. Frantically she started calling for me, "Billy?" I could hear the stress in her voice, but I didn't move.

She ran towards the backyard, still shouting "Billy!" I waited a little longer. I didn't want her to know about my hideout, but it was hard. I hated to worry her. Finally, she moved around the far corner of the house. On the verge of panic, I heard her scream "Billy, where are you?" I jumped up and ran towards the driveway. She was half into her fourth yell when she saw me. The worry on her face changed to relief. I was safe.

Both of my parents sat me down for a talk later that night. They explained to me that when I had thrown the fork, the pointy end had landed first. Its tomato encrusted tines had sunk all the way to the fork's base and into my attacker's left thigh. He later described the "thunk" sound it had made when it hit and how he'd reached down with both hands to carefully grab the handle. Then with a quick jerk, he had yanked it out. He described his shocked horror as four distinct trickles of blood lazed their way down his leg. This of course explained why he hadn't chased me down. Apparently, it's hard to run when you have a fork jabbed in your flesh.

I don't remember much more than that. I was glad I didn't get in trouble for throwing the fork. My actions had been deemed self-defense. My relationship with my brother was not perceptibly different in the following days. But being the youngest in a dysfunctional household, the proverbial shit rolled downhill. Whenever anyone needed to take their frustrations out on someone, I was the easiest target. I don't know if I was a pretty normal kid who's being a baby to even write about all this, or if everything I experienced was genuine abuse. It's so easy to say, "Well, I know there are other people who have it worse, so I can't complain." But today I wonder if those people who, "Had it so much worse," also look back and say, "Well, I know there are other people who had it worse, so I can't complain." Where do we draw that line? I don't know.

Chapter 12

How Many Swings

When I was eight, my dad gifted me a toolbox. Opening it, I found an assortment of his old tools inside; a couple of screwdrivers, a mostly complete socket set, and best of all, one of his old hammers. I remember picking up the hammer and looking it over. On the top area where the head attaches to the handle, I saw that he had driven a big nail alongside the typical wedge. He'd done it so the well-worn wood would stay tight, preventing the head of the hammer from flying off unexpectedly. Though old, it still had a lot of swings left in it. I eventually learned to drive nails with that hammer. And over the next 35 years, I built more projects with it than I can count.

Then one day, I heard a knock at the front door. It was my neighbor. A fence behind his house had fallen down and he was wondering if he could borrow a hammer to put it back together. Without thinking, I went into the garage and grabbed the old hammer. I barely noticed how smooth its handle had become through all the additional years of wear. I didn't think about how I had taken such good care of it, or that my dad's repair had held for all those years. Making my way back to the door, I handed the hammer over and didn't think anymore about it. Except to ask how long he might need it. A couple of hours was the answer, so I told him that was fine. Then I added, if I wasn't there when he came back, just leave the hammer on the garden table outside.

Soon after, I left my house to go run some errands. When I got home, I was quick to look and happy to find that the old hammer was sitting on the table. I walked over to it and grabbed the handle just as I'd done thousands of times before. I started to turn back towards the garage to put it away. That's when the sharp spiny shards dug into my fingers. Looking down in surprise I saw that the old wooden handle, so smooth and comfortable only hours before, was now battered and splintered. Actual chunks of the old hickory were missing, looking as if the neighbor had somehow driven nails with the handle instead of the head. Continuing the examination, my eyes were drawn to the nail-pulling side where a chunk of the claw was broken off. And then, already knowing what the answer would be, I gave it a gentle shake. The metal head of the hammer shifted side to side on its handle, tell-tale evidence that the repair my dad had made all those years ago was now undone.

Carrying the hammer like a badly wounded animal, I ran to the garage. Grabbing a 200-grit sheet of sandpaper, I started working the handle, but it was no use. I would've had to sand away so much that the entire feel of the tool would've been changed. And no amount of sanding could have fixed the splits or gouges. Setting the old hammer on my workbench, I thought about what to do.

After doing some research, I decided to give the hammer a second life. I ordered a new stiletto brand handle for it, and when it arrived, I carefully followed the instructions. I had to customize the handle a little to make it fit the old hammerhead, but eventually, everything went together. I was so excited to try it out, joyful to have overcome the misfortune that had been dealt me. I went outside to try a couple of nails, and the first one drove beautifully. But on the second strike of the second nail, the new wooden handle splintered and the whole head of the hammer flew off.

Gathering the pieces once again, I set it all on my workbench and left it sitting there for a few more months. I considered what it all might mean and what lesson was hiding in this experience. I felt like the hammer was teaching me about how we shouldn't take things for granted. Or maybe how something can mean so much to one person, but to another, it's just a sad old hammer.

Eventually, I started to feel like the hammer broke the second time because it didn't want to give me another chance. I'd broken our trust when I left it in the hands of someone who didn't love it the way I always had. What had started as sadness slowly turned to shame; shame that I hadn't had the foresight to protect the hammer. And that's when I realized that even if I were able to repair it, I'd always think of this. Picking up the head of the hammer and its old handle for the last time, I walked across the shop and dropped it all in the trash.

That hammer lived a long and useful life, but sometimes things reach a point where they're just used up. And when that day finally comes, sometimes the only thing left to do is say goodbye.

That said, I needed a hammer, so the next time I was at Home Depot, I went over to the hammer rack, grabbed one that would do the job, checked out, and brought it home. I tried it out, and it delivered a performance that matched its $18 price tag. I didn't feel any excitement about it. It was just a hammer.

Fast forward a few weeks and a buddy of mine asked if I could help him build some shelving in his garage. I said, of course. I was always happy to help on a project like that. So, the next weekend we built all of his shelving. He offered to pay me for my time, but I declined. He looked at me and said, "I thought you might say that," and then he handed me a package. Opening it up, I found the biggest, baddest, heaviest, gnarly, framing hammer I had ever seen!

"Are you serious?" I asked.

"Yeah, it's all yours," he answered.

Just looking at it, you could tell it was expensive, at least $100, probably more. It was the kind of tool I would never buy for myself, but any craftsman would dream of having. I thanked him and told him the story about how I'd just lost my favorite hammer.

Then, a few days later, another friend of mine was lamenting over how he had left one of his hammers on a job site and was going to have to buy a new one. Casually, I walked over to the $18 hammer that I had purchased at the big box store and said, "Would you like this one?"

"What? Really?" he asked.

"Absolutely," I said, "it's all yours!"

He was so excited about that $18 hammer. He went on and on about how it was exactly what he needed.

So, I lost a hammer, bought a cheap replacement hammer, received an incredible hammer as a gift, then passed on the $18 dollar hammer to another friend who totally loved it. Maybe the universe does know what it's doing.

Chapter 13

Crying Over Spilled Milk

"Gawd damned son of a bitch," my grandfather howled.

I sat in silence, too scared to stop the large puddle of milk as it steadily marched towards the edge of the table.

Grandmother threw her napkin on it. "Oh, it's alright," she said in a tone that made it clear: it wasn't actually alright.

"Real fucking nice! Way to go," grandfather continued, but I had stopped listening.

My mom had told me the stories about my grandfather; about how he grew up on a farm during the Great Depression; and about his Navy days fighting the Nazis in WWII. How he'd almost become a pro baseball player but had to give up the dream to support his family.

He found a job that paid well and worked there for 50 years. He never missed a day but apparently, hated every minute of it. His life was something to be both admired and pitied, for it had made him a hard man.

Noticing that I'd stopped paying attention, my grandfather slammed his fist on the table. Then he threw back his chair and stood up, cursing like a don from a mafia movie as he stood over me menacingly.

I was afraid, but as I looked up at him, something my second grade teacher, Mrs. Williams had just taught us popped into my head.

"Don't cry over spilled milk," she said. "Don't make a big deal out of little things; it's not worth it."

My young brain put it together. This is what she'd meant.

It was a small thing, but here was my grandfather, the big bad war veteran, "crying over spilled milk."

I couldn't help it; I started to laugh.

The storm of rage clouded around him, and he rained all over me. Oh, my goodness, to see his face! But the angrier he got, the harder I laughed. It was so funny to me.

Finally, my grandma emitted a disapproving sigh and left the room in a huff.

Losing some of his steam, he shouted, "Now you've ruined dinner for your grandmother, too. She worked on that all afternoon!"

He stormed out behind her, leaving me and my mom alone in the dining room.

Once they were gone, my mom and I finished cleaning up the spilled milk and sat down for dinner. I picked up my fork and started eating a slice of grandma's famous meatloaf, and it was delicious. Maybe even the best ever, since it was now being enjoyed in such good company.

I could write an entire book on the dysfunction and meanness of my grandparents. This is only a small example of the unhealthy behaviors they displayed. But ultimately, they taught me an incredible lesson. Years later, at 18 years old, I had been hit with one of their all too familiar attacks. But rather than engage, I just walked out the front door and left. As I drove, I realized that I didn't need to subject myself to their abuse anymore. I'd done everything to try and please them, to try and get them to be my friends, or even just be nice to me. But nothing worked because that was the game. There wasn't anything I could do because they fed on my trying. They fed on my failure. Their objective was to keep me on my heels and make me feel as though it was never going to be enough. That is the currency of the bully, convincing you that you're the problem. I don't know how, but all of that became clear as I drove. That day, I decided I was never going to visit them again. And I didn't. No letters, no phone calls, I didn't even go to the funerals when they eventually passed away. I never interacted with either of them ever again, and I have no regrets about it. It was the most difficult, but perhaps the most valuable lesson they ever could have taught me.

Chapter 14

The Short Bus

As a kid, I missed a lot of school because of my heart condition. So understandably, I fell behind in my studies. The medical issues alone would have been tough, but additional struggles arose in second grade. One day our teacher, Mrs. Williams asked everyone to hold up their dominant hands. Most of the kids raised their right hands and a couple lifted their left hands, but I sat there not knowing what to do. So, I didn't raise either hand. She asked me which hand I favored, but I didn't know. Then she asked me which hand was my right and which was the left, but I didn't know that either. All the other kids laughed and pointed at me, so she quieted them down and moved on with the class. But she was curious about this, so later that day she gave us all a writing assignment. I didn't know it at the time, but she was watching me closely to see if there was anything out of the ordinary. It only took her a few minutes to see there was a problem.

Mrs. Williams scheduled a meeting with my mother and met with her to explain what she'd found. She noticed that as I wrote, certain letters would be scrawled out with my left hand, but for others, I would switch to my right hand, sometimes alternating back and forth several times to complete a single word. Her best guess as to why this was happening was that I had taught myself to write while sitting alone in a hospital bed. Without supervision, there had been no one there to encourage me to select a dominant hand, so I hadn't. The good news was that I was wonderfully ambidextrous. The bad news was that my switch style of writing was exceedingly slow. Her concern was that if my handedness were left un-remedied, I'd fall even further behind the other students. She recommended special education classes, which meant that every day, for part of the day, I'd be leaving my regular class to go to a different classroom. My mom asked a few questions and then agreed to the plan. My self-esteem plummeted. All the kids referred to the special ed room as the place the "dumb kids" went. Now I wouldn't just be the "sick kid," I'd be the "dumb kid" too. True to my prediction, within days of starting special ed, I was ostracized.

Despite this, the special ed classes themselves weren't so bad. They actually gave me a measure of freedom few kids had. For example, two days per week the school district arranged for a small bus to come to my elementary school to pick me up. It was entirely up to me if I stayed at school or went on the bus. It would come for me either way. On the days I did go, I often wondered why I was the only kid who ever got on the bus but didn't think much more about it. The driver would take me to a special facility that was 20 minutes away.

Once there, a specialist would work with me one on one. I'm not sure why they had me in this program. All they ever did was take me to the indoor pool and watch me swim. I'd paddle around for as long as I liked, and the teacher would observe. Occasionally she'd ask me questions, then write in her notebook. I didn't know how this was helping me, but it was way better than being in school. So, I went most of the time. But one day when I arrived at the facility, my specialist was not yet available, so the receptionist asked me to wait.

The waiting room was geometrically unusual, not a typical square, more hexagonal. At each corner, the walls would alternate with windows, allowing natural light to brighten the inside. The bench I chose to sit on was next to one of these windows. A little girl was playing in a sandbox right outside, her back leaning against the other side of the glass. I leaned in close to see what she was doing. Over her shoulder I could see a small shovel and pail in front of her. I watched with envy, wishing I could go out and play, too. Looking past her, I saw that the area she was in had a small playground slide, an all-steel tricycle and a few toys scattered around. But as I watched more, something began to feel strange. I wondered: Where were the other kids? Why was there no teacher with her? Why hadn't they ever taken me out to play in this area? As I was pondering, the little girl turned her head slightly and spied me through the glass. Her shovel and pail now forgotten, she slowly turned around to face me directly.

We sat looking at each other with only the window separating us. Her blond hair was pulled back in two neat ponytails, and her eyes were bright and friendly. But something was terribly wrong. Her upper lip was flayed open, a slit reaching up so far it split part of her nose in half. A steady stream of stringy drool oozed uncontrollably from her lower lip. Bits of sand coagulated in it as it slowly made its way to the pool of saliva that had accumulated on her dress. I'd never seen such a thing, and I was horrified.

We continued looking at each other like this for a few seconds, until she tried to say something. "Urghhh gthh ffff," she strained. I sat frozen, clueless as to how to react. She tried again more emphatically, "UrgGGGgg TSSSFFFF!" The words were indecipherable to me. Her cleft palette prevented her from making the sounds necessary for speech, but as I sat looking through the glass at her, something clicked. Something that chilled me even more than her deformity. I realized that her mind was completely intact. She was looking at me, looking at her, and she was aware that I was shocked.

This made me feel sick in a way I'll never be able to put into words. She knew that when people saw her, they felt ill.

Just then, her eyes softened, a resigned acceptance washed across her face, as if she were thinking, "At least one person knows I'm in here."

Slowly, I raised my hand and placed it against the glass. She sat there looking at me for a few more seconds, then she raised her hand to meet mine. We pressed our hands together, separated by the glass, and held them there for a few moments. I smiled at her, and she tried her best to return it. Then, her hand dropped, she turned her back to me again, and returned to her pail and shovel. I looked out across the playground again, but this time with new eyes.

This wasn't a playground at all; it was a cage. The place where kids who couldn't be in regular school went to be forgotten. That's why I was the only one who ever got on the little bus. No one else at my regular school was like me. None of them were like her. We were the ones who got swept under the rug, the dumb and the deformed.

Just then my specialist arrived and took me to the pool to swim, but I no longer felt any joy as I paddled around. It had ceased to be a cool refreshing experience. In my imagination the water had turned into a giant puddle of drool.

That was the last time I ever went to the facility, the last day of being evaluated while I swam, and I never got on a short bus again.

* * *

A few years later, I went to play at my friend Ian's house. We'd just gotten up on top of his jungle gym when I heard "Urghhh gthh ffff" coming from across his backyard. I looked at him and asked, "What was that?"

"Nothing," he said uncomfortably. "It's just my cousin."

I was about to respond, "I didn't know you had a cousin," but was cut off by a much louder, "UrgGGGgg TSSSFFFF!"

Looking across the yard, I saw a young girl with shoulder length blond hair and a cleft palette walking towards us with a long string of spittle dangling from her lower lip. The same girl I had met at special ed.

She walked to the base of the jungle gym, then looked up at us and motioned with her hands saying, "UrgGGG ahhh?"

To my surprise, Ian understood what she was saying because he answered.

"No, why don't you go inside and play with your dolls instead!"

She got a sad look on her face, then motioned again towards the jungle gym pleading, "Pfteee Eeeannn?" (Please Ian)

Ian said, "If you want to play up here, first you have to clean up all of the dog poop" (one of his daily chores).

This seemed to cheer her up, and for the next 10-15 minutes, she dutifully went around the yard with a shovel and a bucket, scooping up all the poop. Eventually she returned and asked again if she could play with us. But Ian assigned her a different task, saying that she could play with us only after she'd done this new thing. This continued for a while until she finally realized that no matter what she did, he was never going to allow her to join us. She started crying and ran into the house.

I looked at Ian and asked, "Why can't she play with us?"

"Because…" his response trailed off.

But I finished his sentence in my head. Because she's one of those kids. One of the kids who gets swept under the rug.

A little later Ian and I rode our bicycles to my house, but only a few minutes after we'd arrived, my mom came out and said that Ian's mom had called and that he was in big trouble. His mom had told my mom about how Ian had treated his cousin.

At first my mom was furious, and said, "I can't believe Billy would do this. I'm putting him on restriction."

But Ian's mom stopped her and said, "Oh no, it was only Ian. Billy wasn't mean to her."

So, Ian went home and spent the next two weeks on restriction. While I sat home and received no punishment because I hadn't done anything.

But that was the problem; I hadn't done anything.

I may not have joined in, but I didn't stand up for her either. And sitting passively by is almost as bad as being the one doing the tormenting. My punishment has been the regret I feel to this day because I didn't stand up for her.

Often in life we find ourselves in situations where we don't know what to do. All we can do is react as best we can in that moment. And sometimes the way we react isn't perfect. This is how we learn. What's important is to reflect on how we could handle those situations differently if they were to happen again. Life has a tendency to repeat itself, and should it repeat, the next time you'll be more prepared to handle it.

Chapter 15

We're Going to Disneyland

It was circa 1986, and a great day because our family was going to Disneyland! My parents and siblings were busily loading the car, but I was ready long before them.

"Mom, mom, come on, let's go," I said, eager for the trip to be underway. But my urging backfired since seeing an idle child was Mom's cue to assign a task. Handing me a bottle of Windex and a roll of paper towels she said, "Why don't you go out and clean all the car's windows inside and out. And we're not leaving until they're spotless." One of my brothers smiled and gave me the "haha" look.

I took the cleaning supplies and sluggishly walked out to the car, all my nine-year-old excitement about Disneyland gone. I looked at our station wagon and its endless windows with dread. "Spotless," I thought. This was going to take forever. I sat down in the front passenger seat and unenthusiastically started to wipe the inside of the front windshield.

Just then my dad walked out of the garage with an armload of gear: icebox, towels, hats, sunscreen, and other such doodads. Everything a good father packs for a family trip. He threw the supplies into the trunk of the car then said, "Great idea Billy! I'm glad to see you taking more initiative." He didn't know that I was actually performing a busy work assignment of the highest order, but I smiled at him, accepting the praise. A few extra brownie points never hurt. Then without another word, he walked over took a big fistful of paper towels from me, and started helping with the windows. I was elated to have help on this monumental task but fearful that if Mom saw him helping, she might tell him to stop. So, I started cleaning as quickly as I could, hoping we could finish before she noticed what was happening. I was wiping as fast as my nine-year-old hands could fly, but when I looked over at my dad, he was moving so fast his hands were almost blurry. He literally cleaned every other window, inside and out, before I'd finished the inside of the front windshield. And I'd had a head start! It seemed impossible, but he'd done it. I examined his work; it was spotless. Then he showed me how to roll the windows down part ways so I could clean the top part of the glass that went into the rubber gasket. He'd done that on all the windows he'd cleaned, too.

Once he finished, he strode off to the garage to grab more "who knows what's it's" for our journey. I love my dad. He taught me so many important life lessons without even realizing he was doing it, and what he taught me that day was clear. In life there will be things you don't want to do: emptying the garbage, washing dishes, or cleaning windows. But whether the task is fun or not, these things need to be done, so get to work. And since they have to be done anyway, you might as well do it as quickly as possible. Then you can get back to doing something you'd rather be doing, like going to Disneyland.

Chapter 16

Playing With Fire

During the summer between fifth and sixth grade, I went to hang out with my friend Steve almost every day. Our favorite thing to do was play war in the trees and bushes around his house. So, when Steve's parents decided they wanted to install a below ground swimming pool, they made us an offer. If we would agree to dig out a big hole where the pool would eventually go, his parents would wait until the next summer to move forward with the installation. In the meantime, they said we could use the hole to build an underground bunker to play war in. We of course jumped at the chance. Steve and his brother did a lot of the work, but a bunch of the neighborhood kids helped out. And in just a few weeks, the hole was all dug out. We scrounged old materials from a nearby field to cover the hole. Then we lay tarps down over the wood and spread a thin layer of dirt over that to camouflage everything. The "bunker" was complete. 5′ deep, 10′ wide, 15′ long, kidney shaped, with one entrance and two different levels (for the shallow and deep ends).

It was lots of fun to play in, but for Steve it wasn't enough. He wanted to make the game more real. So, one day he started playing with fire and wanted to make his own napalm. He experimented with any combustible materials or flammable chemicals that he could find. The fort became his impromptu laboratory for conducting these "tests." It seemed harmless, and Steve claimed to know what he was doing, but I always stayed outside while he was burning things. I didn't even feel comfortable striking matches, so I sure as heck wasn't going down there where the fire was.

After a few weeks, Steve decided it was time to improve his concoctions by adding gasoline into the mix. I was visiting when he tested this out for the first time. As usual, I sat right outside the entrance to watch. He began by lighting a small brush fire on the floor of the fort. Then he picked up a large plastic bottle filled with gasoline and slowly poured it onto the flames. The fuel was so combustible that the flames raced up the stream into the full bottle, and then exploded. The entire interior of the fort was instantly engulfed in flames!

I leaped backward in fear; the heat was searing even though I was several yards away. In complete panic, I ran away from the fort. I could hear him screaming behind me, but I was too afraid to stop. I got to my bicycle and was about to jump on when my brain kicked back on. My instant thought was, "What if he burns to death?" I hesitated for a second, not knowing what to do, then I heard him scream again, "Billy, help!"

I turned around and sprinted back towards the fort. When I got there, flames were coming out of the entrance, and I couldn't see Steve at all. I dropped to my knees and started throwing dirt through the opening as fast as I could. The fire died down a little and I could see Steve huddled in the deep end behind a wall of flames four feet tall. He was completely frozen and in shock. I could see the fire reflecting in his glazed over eyes, like a scene from a horror movie. It was surreal. I kept throwing dirt until a gap appeared in the flames. As soon as Steve saw this opportunity, he made a break for it, nearly bowling me over in his rush to escape. Once he was safely outside with me, we joined forces, throwing dirt wildly until the fire was completely out.

With a feeling of relief, we stood up and shakily looked at each other. Then he moaned, "My leg," and started to limp his way toward the house.

I walked beside him, trying my best to help. A few steps later he began to whimper, then he quickened his steps. Whimpers turned to shouts, and he began to run. Before we made it to the backdoor of his house, the adrenaline had fully worn off and he broke into a full sprint, screaming maniacally as he went. I tried to follow him inside, but he locked me out.

I went around to the front of the house, but the front door was locked, too.

I knocked and knocked but he didn't answer. I could hear him screaming inside and I didn't know what to do, so I kept knocking. Finally, he opened the door. His face was transformed by the pain, cheeks streaked by tears. Between the screams he shouted, "Go home!" Then he slammed the door in my face.

Still not knowing what to do or how I could help, I finally walked over to my bicycle and rode home. When I arrived, my mom instantly knew something was wrong, but I said nothing and went to my room. It wasn't until she got a call from Steve's parents a few hours later that she learned what had happened. Apparently, Steve had been rushed to the emergency room. The doctors diagnosed second and third-degree burns on large swaths of his legs. It would take multiple skin grafts over several months to repair the damage. While recovering, he was instructed to keep his burns out of the sunlight for two years while the skin regenerated.

I never did see his wounds up close. We never talked about what happened that day, and we never played war again. The one time we did run into each other, he flipped me off from across the street and shouted, "Billy's a fag!" I just shook my head and continued walking.

I still wonder about his behavior. Maybe he somehow blamed me for the accident. Or maybe seeing me just brought up painful memories.

I know for myself, I have regrets about the accident. I knew full well it was dangerous, and I'd tried numerous times to get him to stop, but he wouldn't listen. Short of being a tattletale, I had no way to head off the disaster. I feared losing his friendship if I got him in trouble, so I didn't say anything. But in the end, he got burned, and I lost him as a friend anyway. Maybe I should have said something. The other thing I really didn't like was that my initial reflex had been to run away. Yes, I was panicked and experiencing something new, and fire is scary, I get it. But I didn't like that self-preservation took precedence over a friend in need. It felt ugly and selfish, and I never wanted to feel that way again. I think this incident planted many seeds for the person I'd eventually become.

Years later when I began seriously pursuing entertainment as a career, one of our signature bits was one where I'd light my legs on fire and then juggle a chainsaw that was on fire. I performed it hundreds of times, each time getting a small taste of what Steve experienced that day.

Chapter 17

Mom Dog Vs The Pitbull

When I was a kid, we had three friendly dogs: Diamond, who was half German Shepard and half Australian Shepard; Heart, an energetic Collie; and "The Mom Dog," a long-haired stray who showed up in our yard one day with five puppies in tow. We found homes for all the puppies but kept Mom Dog because she was a sweetheart. We had a big backyard for them to run around in, but my mom and I would take them for regular walks as well. I would always take Diamond because he was my dog, and my mom would walk the other two. We'd set off on our usual route, a loop around my elementary school that we'd easily taken 100+ times before. I loved these outings and would look forward to the many familiar landmarks along the way. There was the old plum tree that I'd sometimes pick fruit from and the little old lady who obsessively watered her lawn in an old, faded bathrobe. She would always wave at us, and we'd of course wave back. Then about midway through the walk, there was a house that I liked. Its front yard was completely overgrown with broad-leafed ivy which made it look like a tropical jungle. This feeling was reinforced by the fact that we had never once seen anyone there. Only the faint glow of light through the curtained windows gave away that someone did indeed live there. But on this particular evening, as we were passing the Jungle House, I heard a loud slam. Looking up I briefly saw a big pit bull with short white fur charging towards us, but then he disappeared into the sea of ivy that separated the house from the sidewalk.

I couldn't see him anymore, but I knew exactly where he was because the ivy shook violently as he tore through it. I was struck by how similar it looked to a torpedo zipping through the water. I judged by the movement of the ivy that the pit bull was going to come out right where my mom and our other two dogs were. And sure enough, the dog burst from the undergrowth just a few feet in front of them. Heart and Mom Dog wagged their tails in anticipation of meeting this new stranger, but the pit bull had other plans. In an instant he clamped his massive jaws around Mom Dog's throat, slamming her to the ground in the process. Chaos erupted! My dog was barking maniacally, trying to get into the fight. I was seven years old and skinny as they come, so it was all I could do to keep from being pulled off my feet. My mom struggled to control Heart who was trying to run away, while at the same time interceding in the raging fight between Mom Dog and the pit bull. I watched as they struggled, wanting to help, wanting to stop it, but helpless to do anything. The fight continued for what felt like an eternity, and eventually, Mom Dog stopped struggling. She hung limply in the pit bull's jaws, but even then, he didn't let her go. I began to wonder if this dog was going to systematically kill all of our dogs one by one. Things were desperate.

But there was one thing no one could have anticipated. My mom was a strong woman. Standing 5'11", she'd worked hard all her life, and she for damn sure wasn't going to stand by and do nothing while he killed our dog. So, she reached down with her one free hand, grabbed the pit bull by his collar, and literally lifted him and Mom Dog off of the ground. She held them in the air at arm's length. Once the pit bull was off the ground, he panicked and released his grip on Mom Dog, but my mom didn't release her grip on him. He struggled to get free, wriggling like a fish as it dangles from the end of a line. Still holding him high she shouted, "Come get your damn dog!" Moments later, a man wearing only a wife beater and boxer shorts came running out of the house. But by now my mom's strength had started to wane, and the pit bull's back legs made contact with the ground. He leapt violently, trying to break her grip, but she still held him half in the air.

Finally, the dog's owner grabbed his dog and pulled him towards the house. Despite this, the pit bull still fought madly, trying to attack. When the man got his dog inside and slammed the door, we turned our attention to Mom Dog. We were overjoyed to see that she was alert. Trying to catch her breath, she coughed several times, a deep bronchial sound I'd never heard before, but she was breathing. My mom combed through her thick fur and found four deep wounds where each of the pit bull's canine teeth had sunk into her flesh. If it weren't for all that fur, she likely would've had more severe injuries. My mom started up the driveway to talk to the owners about what had happened but suddenly my heart condition flared up. Any surprising or stressful situation tended to set it off, so instead, we set off for home so she could get me to the emergency room.

I'd been diagnosed with supraventricular tachycardia at a young age, but it wasn't a normal case. While in an episode, my heart rate would frequently soar into the high 200's, and one time an EKG operator got a recording that showed it breaking 300. The usual medications were ineffective at regulating it, so anytime I had an episode, it was life-threatening. We got home and put the dogs away, then it was into the car for the familiar drive to Kaiser Hospital. We always went straight to the front of the line without waiting, just as my cardiologist had instructed. In the hundreds of visits we made, I don't ever remember having to wait. Even when there were lots of people there, they always had a bed ready. But as much as I hated it, this was my normal. I was at the hospital two times every week just for blood tests, and each episode of arrhythmia triggered an extra visit. On this day, they gave me an IV, and administered the typical cocktail of meds, and an hour later my heart snapped back to normal.

Once they were sure it was fixed, I was discharged, and we drove back home.

After we'd arrived and put antibiotics on Mom Dog's wounds, my mom sat me down to talk about what had happened.

Mom: How do you feel about what happened today?

Me: Angry!

Mom: That's understandable; it was a terrible situation.

Me: Yeah.

Mom: So, what do you think we should do?

Me: I don't know. What can we do?

Mom: Well, we could call animal control, and they would probably come take the dog away and put it to sleep.

Me: Yeah, let's call animal control!

Mom: It's so strange. How many times do you think we've walked by that house?

Me: Lots!

Mom: And how many times have we ever seen that dog?

Me: Never, not once.

Mom: I didn't even know they had a dog, so they must be pretty good about keeping him locked up.

Me: Yeah.

Mom: And I bet they love their dog, just like we love our dogs.

Me: Yeah.

Mom: How would you have felt if we lost Mom Dog today?

Me: Awful!

Mom: So that's probably how they would feel if animal control came and took away their dog I bet.

Me: Yeah.

Mom: They're probably sitting at home right now, worried sick that that's exactly what's going to happen.

Me: Yeah, they're probably as scared as we were.

Mom: Yeah, so what do you think? Should we call animal control, or should we go over there and tell them that our dog is going to be okay and that they don't need to worry because we're not going to have their dog put down? It's up to you.

Me: Let's tell them our dog is okay and that their dog is going to be okay, too.

Mom: Okay, let's go.

So, we drove to the Jungle House, pulled into the driveway, and explained to the family everything my mom and I had talked about. The people were very apologetic about the incident and grateful for our visit. They had been worried about what would happen. Then my mom said good night and we went our separate ways.

We continued to walk that same route for several years without ever seeing the pit bull or the people again.

* * *

Four or five years later, my dad rented a commercial space to run our family sign shop out of. He'd only been able to afford it by splitting the space with a local locksmith, but after a few months, the locksmith flaked and stopped paying his half of the rent. My parents managed to cover it on their own for two months, but they were sinking fast. They called the property manager and asked to be let out of the lease.

The property manager said, "I understand the situation and am terribly sorry, but the owner of this property doesn't let anyone out of their leases. I've been working with him for over ten years, and I've never seen it happen."

My parents said they understood, but asked if the property manager would please ask the owner anyways.

The property manager said, "Sure, I will, but don't get your hopes up."

A few days later a big fancy car that we didn't recognize pulled up in front of the shop, and a well-dressed man stepped out. He walked into the shop and introduced himself to my parents. He was the owner of the property and said that he'd wanted to come personally and tell us that he was letting us out of the lease.

My dad graciously thanked him, then asked, "You know the property manager mentioned that you don't typically let anyone out of their leases, so why are you letting us out?"

The man looked at my parents for a moment and said, "A number of years ago our dog broke through the front door of our house and attacked some people who were just walking by. Later that night they came back, and to our relief, told us that they were not going to have our dog destroyed. This became even more meaningful because only a few months after that incident our dog became very ill and had to be put down. My family has always been grateful for those extra few months with him."

My parents looked at him in shock and said "Oh my god! How in the world did you know it was us?"

The owner smiled kindly and said, "When you came to our house that night, the sign on the side of your truck said, 'Berry Signs.' So, when I found out you had moved into one of my buildings, I had already planned to come down here one day to say thank you. You just gave me the excuse I needed to stop by." Then he reached into his pocket and pulled out a sheet of paper. "It is my honor to release you from this lease obligation," and he tore the paper in half. He handed the torn pages to my father and said, "If there's ever anything else I can do for you, please don't hesitate to ask." He turned around and walked out of the shop.

Chapter 18

For my Mom's Birthday

On my mom's 38th birthday, she picked me up from elementary school, and when I got in the car I asked her, "So, what do you want to do for your birthday?"

She thought about it for a moment, then said, "I would like to buy you a new soccer ball."

I looked down at the tattered soccer ball sitting in my lap; the soccer ball I took everywhere with me. Of course I thought it would be nice to have a new one, but I just as quickly retorted, "No, it's your birthday. We have to get something nice for you!"

She thought about it a little more, then said, "No really, getting you a soccer ball would be the best present I could imagine."

The next thing I knew, we were at a small sporting goods store, picking out a new soccer ball.

I could not tell you anything about that soccer ball today, but I remember her actions like it was yesterday. She was always teaching me little lessons like this, helping me to notice things about the world I might otherwise have missed.

I wonder if instead of receiving presents on our birthdays, we gave them out instead. How might that change the world?

Chapter 19

Whiskey

"Oh no," my dad gasped.

I strained my eight-year-old body against the seatbelt, trying to see out the front windshield. In the car's headlights, there were two strange lumps moving in the street. One of the lumps reached a furry white paw up towards the sky before spasmodically launching backward.

As the car moved closer, I could see that the paw belonged to my tuxedo cat, Whiskey. He was trying to run. Lying next to him was an orange cat I didn't recognize. Instantly, I realized what had happened. Whiskey was chasing the other cat out of our yard, something I had seen him do many times. But this time, as they'd entered the street, both had been hit by a passing car.

My parents jumped out of our car and ran to the cats. Dad carefully lifted Whiskey off the pavement, carrying him delicately. Then he set Whiskey in the middle of the backseat and climbed in beside him.

Mom was bringing the orange kitty too, so I climbed into the hatchback area of our station wagon to make room. She set the orange kitty in the back seat beside Whiskey, then started driving us to the 24-hour emergency animal hospital. She told my dad, "It'll take 30 minutes to get there."

I looked at my dad's profile and he was completely focused as he worked on the cats. A former serviceman in Vietnam, he was the most capable of us to help.

Whiskey started meowing in distress, but it was a half meow-half gasp. The sound pierced my heart. I was hanging half over the back of the seat so I could see everything.

The orange cat was lying on his left side like he was asleep. But blood poured freely from his mouth forming a deep puddle under his head and chest. In the darkness, it looked like Hawaiian Punch, only more viscous.

Whiskey then started writhing erratically. My dad spoke to him gently, "It's okay buddy, you're gonna be alright. Just hang on."

I couldn't bear it and dropped down on the dirty beige carpet in the cargo area. I started praying out loud, "Please God, I'll do anything you ever ask. Just please don't take him. Please God, I'll do anything."

"The orange cat is gone," Dad said.

Time seemed to stand still after my dad delivered that news.

Through tears, I prayed louder, "Please God, don't let Whiskey die!"

Whiskey's cries became less frequent and turned to a gurgling sound. Then he went quiet.

"We're almost there," Mom said.

We pulled in and she double parked in front of the entrance. My parents grabbed the cats and sprinted inside. I followed them, taking care not to step in the blood all over the laminate floor.

I heard my mom say to the receptionist, "Money is no object; save him."

A veterinarian quickly appeared and surveyed the scene. I already knew it was bad, but the look on his face told me it was very bad. He took Whiskey from my dad and disappeared through a big set of white double doors.

There was nothing we could do now but wait.

Eventually, the big white door opened again, and the veterinarian slowly stepped out. His shoulders were slumped, and he didn't look at us right away.

"I'm very sorry," he said.

Mom began to cry, and through her tears asked, "Was there nothing to be done?"

"His lungs filled with blood," the doctor replied. "There was nothing we could do."

No one said it, but I realized Whiskey had drowned in his own blood. The horror of what he suffered shattered my mind. This was death.

* * *

What happened that night scarred me deeply. And anytime I thought about Whiskey, the entire event would replay in my mind like a horrible movie. But it was worse because I would relive the moment as if it were happening all over again.

And that continued for over three decades, bringing anguish with it each time.

Eventually, I learned to avoid many of the triggers, and the flash-backs lessened, but I could never get rid of them completely. I didn't even think of it as something that could be fixed. I had accepted it the same as I'd accepted my eye color and shoe size, just another fact of life.

But one day a friend said something that changed everything. She said, "Most people who experience PTSD are holding onto some guilt."

That was the first time I realized I was suffering from PTSD. And it seemed so obvious once she'd said it. I had most of the symptoms, but I could never see it for myself. I also experienced the exact guilt she was talking about.

I'd been holding onto the feeling that I hadn't been loving enough towards him while he was alive. After he died, I'd even said, "I'll never forgive myself." And I didn't.

But that promise had prevented me from ever healing or moving past the trauma.

It was the piece of the puzzle I'd been missing.

Now I just needed to forgive myself.

But how could I let it go? It couldn't be that easy.

I thought about it for the next three days.

Then while on a bike ride, this thought came into my head, "Whiskey loved you; he wouldn't want you to suffer like this. He would forgive you."

Like a light switch, I felt everything I'd been hanging onto flow out of me. Years of anguish lifted from my shoulders. Suddenly I felt like I could breathe again.

But was I healed? There was only one way to find out.

When I got home, I went straight to the drawer where I kept all our old family photos. Reaching inside, I pulled out a small cardboard box.

There were three pictures of Whiskey inside. But I'd never been able to look at them before without breaking down.

I slid the lid off and was greeted by that old photo album scent. Then reaching inside I picked up the three photos and started to look at them. I felt a smile lift my cheeks. No panic attack, no tears, no flashbacks; just a beautiful boy.

I couldn't believe it. I didn't feel any sadness. I actually felt happy. Happy for the beautiful life he'd lived, and happy for the many wonderful memories. The memories I'd been unable to access while still suffering from the trauma of his death.

Whiskey's death cracked the foundation everything else was built upon. Yet as simple as it seemed, I only had to realize one tiny thing to let go of 36 years of trauma, guilt, and PTSD. I had to learn to forgive myself.

I'm sharing this because so many people are carrying something like this. Some without even knowing, while others know it well, but they have no idea what to do about it. I want to tell you that when you're ready, that heavy thing on your shoulders can be lifted away. It doesn't have to feel like that forever. Your answers are out there. Don't give up the search for them.

Chapter 20

Black Labrador

Barely visible in the darkness I saw a large black dog on the side of the road. She was lying on her belly awkwardly, and it looked like she'd been hit by a car. I asked my mom to turn around so we could check on her. As we pulled up, I could see through the window that she was a wreck. I turned around in my seat and reached back to open the rear passenger door, and then we called to her to see if she'd climb in. Sensing that we wanted to help, the poor thing dutifully dragged herself toward the car. Her hindquarters had been crushed, both legs trailed uselessly behind her. She made it to the open door and tried to climb in but couldn't. Her left front paw was the only thing she was able to get up onto the seat. My mom reached back and grabbed her by the scruff, and in one heave pulled her in. I closed the door, and we started driving to the emergency animal hospital.

It was an all too familiar journey. Only a few months earlier, we'd raced my cat Whiskey to this same hospital after he'd been hit by a car. On that trip, my dad had been there and done all he could to keep Whiskey alive, but there was too much damage. He didn't make it.

This time it was just me and my mom. My dad wasn't here to take care of the wounded. And since my mom was driving, I was the only one who could help. So, I undid my seatbelt and climbed into the backseat to assess her condition. Thick strands of dark fluid hung from her bottom jaw, which itself dangled unnaturally. Several of her teeth were broken and large patches of fur had been torn away along her left side. She reeked of metallic blood, oil, and asphalt. Every inch of her was matted with gore like she had rolled around on a slaughterhouse floor. Her back legs were twisted beside her in a position that's only possible when everything is broken. I wanted to help her but didn't know how. What could I do? I was only eight years old. Then I realized, she was watching me. I looked into her eyes, and she looked into mine. I saw pain, misery, and fear, but also, I saw trust. I wanted to hug her but was afraid to touch her. We continued along quietly, and though she was suffering terribly, she made no complaints. She was a brave girl. Suddenly the calm atmosphere was shattered as she began to convulse.

I flashed back to Whiskey and thought, "This is what happens before they die."

My recently broken heart broke again; I felt helpless. Her spasms intensified.

This was it.

I prepared myself for her passing. Her spasms became a deep heaving gasp. Her body shook violently. Then she projectile vomited her internal parts onto the seat between us. I looked down in shock at a chicken breast-sized mound of tissue. It was an eerie dark burgundy hue like raw liver.

How was she still alive?

In shock I started saying over and over, "I can smell the blood. I can smell the blood."

My mom answered helplessly from the front seat, "I know, honey."

Finally, we reached the animal hospital, and my mom carried her inside. The doctors immediately took the wounded dog through the big white door.

As we waited for the veterinarian, I expected him to come back and tell us it was useless. That they'd done all they could. That we could have saved her if only we'd done this or that. Just like they'd told us after we'd lost Whiskey.

But 30 minutes later, the doctor came out and said, "We were able to stabilize her. How would you like to proceed?"

Mom asked, "How bad is it?"

The doctor said, "Well, it's pretty bad. If she survives the night, you'll be looking at multiple surgeries to try and fix everything. And you should know, she may never walk again. It's touch and go. Is she your dog?"

My mom said, "No, it's a stray we found."

"We can do whatever you like, but it will be expensive, and I cannot make any promises," the doctor cautiously replied.

My mom thought about it for a few seconds, then turned to me and asked, "What do you want to do?"

I realized she wasn't just asking for my opinion. She was handing the dog's fate entirely over to me. I thought about it for a few seconds.

Then, looking up at the vet I said as evenly as I could, "Let her go. She's suffered enough."

My mom asked, "Are you sure?"

"Yes," I answered.

With resolve the doctor said, "Okay, we'll take care of her. Would you like to take her home to bury?"

My mom looked at me again, so I answered, "No, you can keep her."

Looking at the doctor, she nodded her confirmation of my decision.

He said, "Alright," and left the room.

My mom went to the check-in window, filled out some paper-work, and paid for the treatment. Then we walked out the door.

I never got to see the dog again, but the smell of asphalt and blood has never left me. I can still smell it now as I sit here 30+ years later. When we walked out of the office that night I was changed. When my cat Whiskey died, I'd been a boy with a broken heart. When this dog died, the boy inside me died along with her. From that day on I was an adult, though still too young, small, and lacking in wisdom to actually become a man.

Chapter 21

The Man in the Rusty Chevy

I was ten years old and playing in our front yard when I noticed a stray dog. She was about five houses down from ours, walking in the gutter of our suburban street. Her dangling teats spoke of recent motherhood, and I wondered to myself where her puppies might be. She had that telltale mile-eating trot strays develop when they've been out on their own for a while. I wondered if she was finding enough food. She was just a dark-furred little girl alone in the world, earning a living, and minding her own business. I was about to go inside to find her something to eat, but then I noticed a truck turn onto the street behind her. It was an old Chevy, and it was headed our way. Its body was a mix of rust and patchwork primer gray, with oversized tires and an overly aggressive body lift. As the truck got closer, I could hear the whirr whirr whirr sound that off-road tires make when they're on concrete. Then the hum of the engine turned to a roar as the man at the wheel pushed the gas pedal to the floor. I saw his hands swing clockwise on the wheel swerving the truck into the gutter. The hollow sound of rubber grinding on concrete told me he was riding right up against the curb. I watched helplessly as he closed in on the stray. Then, just as he was about to hit her, I felt the impulse to look away, but I didn't. Shielding myself from her final seconds of life somehow felt disrespectful, so I held my eyes steady, bearing witness to whatever may come. The weight in my belly grew unbearable. But then, by some miracle, she hopped up the curb and the truck passed harmlessly through the space where she had just been standing. The wind from the trucks passing was like a physical blow. It sent her scurrying, with face grimaced and tail tucked.

The truck moved closer to my house, so I could see the driver more clearly. He was light-skinned and shirtless, with dark unkempt hair parted on the left. His hands were stained dark like the ones I've seen on junkyard mechanics.

Two more seconds and the truck blew past, eventually disappearing a few blocks up the way.

Standing in my front yard, just feet from where we'd found Whiskey and the orange cat, all I could think was, "Is that how Whiskey died? Because some lousy piece of shit deliberately ran him over!" My blood boiled at the thought. I had assumed Whiskey's death was an accident. Anyone can accidentally hit a cat. That's just bad luck. But, to witness this man deliberately try and hit the dog made me aware of the possibility. The thought tore my heart from my chest. An indescribable anger rose up in me, and it no longer mattered that he'd missed the dog. What he'd attempted was unforgivable. If at that moment I'd been granted godlike powers, I would have called down lightning and struck the driver dead right there. It was the first time I'd ever wanted to kill; the moment I realized I could be capable of killing if pushed beyond reason. But there was nothing I could do, and nothing happened to that man.

That moment taught me that there are people in this world who just want to destroy. People who take pleasure in doing evil. People who on occasion have to be stopped. That revelation saddened me on that day. But it is also what drives me to protect the ones I love so fiercely. It's why I always root for the underdog, and help others whenever I can. And maybe, if we do enough good things, those things will eventually outpace the evil.

Chapter 22

Broken Glass

When I was a kid, the fastest way to the corner store was to cut across the railroad tracks behind the old apartment complex. There were "no trespassing," signs posted, but undesirable elements still hung out around the area. One of my friends had been robbed on two separate occasions while trying to cross. Despite this, it was the shortest way, and I was with my older brother, so I figured we'd be okay.

We passed through an opening someone had cut in the chain link fence, then we made our way up to the tracks. As I stepped between the rails, I was assailed by the sound of breaking glass and felt my legs sprayed with hot liquid. Looking around I tried to identify where the attack had come from and saw two teenage boys peeking over the top of a six-foot tall concrete wall. My initial impulse was to keep going and just ignore them, but my brother was a hothead, so he yelled angrily at them, "What the hell?" One of the teenagers yelled back something unintelligible, but it was clearly unfriendly because they threw another bottle at us. This one was way off target, so my brother made fun of the guy's terrible throw. Then he started walking towards them. I thought this was a stupid idea, but I walked with him. The saying, "Gotta back your brother's play," popped into mind.

As we approached within 30 to 40 feet of the wall, one of the teenagers casually raised his other hand into sight. In it he held a silver semi-automatic pistol. My brother and I stopped cold as the kid made a show of closing one eye and pointing it at us. My brain was screaming, *Run! Get out of here!* But I didn't move.

I once saw a wild rabbit sit perfectly still when our dogs approached it. They just sniffed him a couple of times before walking away. If that rabbit had run, oh lordy, the chase would have been on. And somehow in this moment, I knew that if we ran, it would be the same. So unflinching, we stared him down, waiting to see what would happen next. An eternity passed before he slowly lowered the gun. Then giving us a look of incredulity, he shook his head side to side as if to say, "You stupid motherfuckers." Then he and his friend ducked their heads behind the wall. That was the last we saw of them.

As we continued on to the store, my fear subsided, only to be replaced with a quiet internalized anger. My initial impulse had been to keep going, to not confront them, just run away from the danger. But no, my brother needed to address their slight and face it head-on. Instead of teaching those kids some lesson, all he'd done was lead us into a situation even more dangerous. We could have been killed, for nothing!

The lesson I learned that day was double-edged. It taught me to walk away and avoid confrontation, which is a valuable and important lesson. In a situation like the one we'd just been in, getting away from the danger is the smartest thing you can do. But I globalized this run-away strategy as a one size fits all philosophy for life, to walk away and avoid all confrontations. In the following years, I zealously employed this tool of avoidance, only to find myself frequently bullied and taken advantage of. There are times when passivity gets you nowhere, and life, being an imposing teacher, would soon teach me this.

Chapter 23

7th Grade Bully

He squared off with me, a look of menace in his eyes. "Give it," he commanded.

I shook my head no, then turned away. Locking my eyes on the open gym locker in front of me, I hoped he'd go away.

Without warning he slugged me in the stomach.

Air exploded out of my 7th grade lungs, and my body crumpled to the ground. As I sat there trying to catch my breath, the bully helped himself to my things. He grabbed my Walkman tape player, some schoolbooks, and my jacket. Then he looked down at me, his 9th grade stature looming large. I hoped he had taken whatever he wanted so he could just leave. But then he said, "Ah, one more thing." Reaching down with his free hand, he grabbed the silver cross that I always wore around my neck. It was a present my mom had gotten me for my birthday. With a quick yank, he broke the chain. Holding it in front of my eyes he said, "I've been wanting one just like this." Then he turned and walked away.

The irony of him stealing the cross wasn't lost on me, but raised Christian, I endeavored to forgive him.

It was my second day of middle school and the end of any academic aspirations. From that day on, school ceased to have anything to do with learning. It was a place to endure, a place to be caged despite having committed no crime. With a sentence that lasted until my 18th birthday, and all I wanted was to do my time and be done with it.

My full attention turned to navigating the complex and illogical social structures of adolescence. I tried to avoid the places where the bullies might be, but they were everywhere. And the bullying worsened over the coming months. Eventually, the truth about my ever-present bruises came out, and my mom enrolled me in a different school. It was a private catholic school right across the street from the middle school I'd been attending, but close as it was, it was far enough away that those bullies stopped hassling me.

Changing schools helped, but it only kicked the problem down the road. I still had no tools for dealing with bullies, and within weeks new bullies appeared.

When avoiding the problem proved impossible, my mom enrolled me in karate classes, no doubt hoping I'd learn to defend myself. I took those for about one year. Then I moved to a different school where a kid had recently been stabbed to death. In response, my mom transferred me to White Tiger Kung Fu classes because they did weapons training. There, I learned the fundamentals of knife defense, grappling, and more striking techniques. And occasionally, if I showed up to those classes early enough, the Thai boxing instructor would still be there and he'd show me some things as well. Honestly, this training didn't change anything, at least not at first. But I continued to take steps toward the solution, and over time, my skills and confidence grew. I never became a black belt, and I'd stand no chance in the UFC, but I became competent enough in self-defense that the bullying eventually stopped. It was my first exposure to the benefits of long term gradual improvement. Many of the most rewarding things in life take years of practice to reach proficiency. So whatever goals you set for yourself, don't give up too easily, tomorrow will be better.

Chapter 24

Truth, Justice & Gummi Bears

I pointed towards the ceiling of our seventh-grade classroom, "That one."

Sister Elsa stared over the top of her glasses; her habit-covered head haloed in yellow, fluorescent light. Slowly she looked up at the red gummi bear stuck to the white popcorn ceiling.

She raised one crooked finger, "You only threw one?"

"Yes," I said nodding, "I didn't throw any of the others."

"Get up," she shouted. "Go stand in front of the class!"

I did as I was told.

When Sister Elsa announced two weeks ago that, "This year for Valentine's Day, the school has done away with traditional card exchange in favor of 'Gummi Grams,'" I never imagined this would be the result.

Sister proceeded to the next desk, repeating her question to the boy who sat behind me. "Did you throw one?"

He squeaked out a timid, "No."

Unconvinced, she pointed her finger at him ominously, "Do you swear it, before God?"

He melted lower in his chair, "I swear."

She glared at him, and her scowl made the cavernous wrinkles in her cheeks look like portals to the underworld. If this was the 15th century, she would undoubtedly torture each and every one of us. But alas, it was 1990 and she can only threaten eternal damnation and detention.

The boy shook visibly under her gaze but was unrelenting.

Eventually satisfied, the angel of death passed him by.

As she made her way to the back of my row, heretic after heretic was undone. Harry and Geoff were sent to wait beside me in judgment. They were known troublemakers, so I was surprised they confessed without lying or trying to get out of it.

Our inquisitor started down the next row, eventually arriving at the desk next to mine.

Its occupant sat calmly, hands piously interlaced around a mountain of gummi bear packages, each with a card attached. Uniquely, her catholic schoolgirl uniform was both tailored & pressed which made her already perfect posture look extra crisp.

Sister Elsa raised her challenge, "Jessica. Tell me now. Did you throw one?"

Jessica looked directly into Sister Elsa's eyes, then in a voice that dripped milk and honey said, "No, Sister Elsa."

"Do you swear it, before God?" sister pressed.

Jessica's obedient blond locks swayed side to side as she shook her head, "I swear, I didn't throw one."

Sister Elsa nodded knowingly then said, "I knew you would not succumb to such childish temptation!"

The inquisition continued, and after every student had endured Sister Elsa's withering gaze, three more guilty boys joined me at the front of the class. All these boys were regular troublemakers. Except for me of course, I rarely got in trouble.

Sister Elsa clicked her tongue disapprovingly as she looked us over, "You will all report to the principal's office for punishment. Dismissed!"

As we began to shuffle out single file, I looked out at all my class-mates' faces who were still seated.

Quite a few of them should have been up here with us; two more boys and at least five of the girls in class were also throwing them while Sister was out of the classroom.

But most notably absent from our lineup was Jessica. She started the whole thing when she threw several gummi bears at Ivan, the boy she liked.

Ivan retaliated and threw them back, but when he did, one of them had landed on my desk.

When I picked it up, I was mortified to find it wet and sticky, instantly realizing he'd licked it before throwing. Gross!

Jumping like it was a snake, the gummi flew out of my hand. But because it was sticky, it clung to my finger on release. This changed its trajectory causing the gummi to fly straight up and stick to the ceiling.

Suddenly every eye was transfixed by the solitary red gummi bear above my desk. At that moment, Satan had planted his seeds of temp-tation. Seconds later, gummi-geddon erupted.

Everyone was licking and sticking as fast as they could! I tried to hide behind my three-subject notebook, but it was futile. Multicol-ored candies were whizzing past from every direction, sticking to everything and everyone. Then I watched as Jessica threw an entire handful of wet gummies straight up, sticking six to seven of them in one shot. Moments later, Sister Elsa returned.

The school janitor would later report that in two minutes, we'd managed to stick over 100 gummi bears to the walls and ceiling of our classroom.

The six of us made our way to the principal's office where we waited for over an hour before we were called in. Once admitted, we the accused stood shoulder to shoulder while the principal made a show of being too busy to notice us. We waited quietly while she organized her desk. Eventually, without looking up she began, "You all know why you're here. Your parents have been notified. You're all suspended for three days. That is all."

I was stunned. I had never been suspended before.

"Good day, gentlemen," she said dismissively.

"Wait, I was innocent," I thought. "When were we going to get a chance to plead our case? Where was the part where I could explain myself and explain everything?"

But the conversation was over. It was a travesty of justice. As we slunk out of her office, I saw my mom in the waiting area. It was the only time I had ever seen her disappointed in me. We walked to the car in silence. On the way home she finally asked, "So, you wanna tell me what happened?"

If only I had received that same chance to explain myself in the principal's office. I never imagined that we would all be suspended, especially without having a chance to defend our actions. It deeply impacted my understanding of justice. I'd seen that a person could be innocent or make an honest mistake, and still be punished along with the guilty. It didn't seem fair.

I'd also seen the guilty get away without even a slap on the wrist. Jessica lied about her involvement, and no one doubted it for a second. She was an outlier who got straight A's, had perfect attendance, and also happened to be the daughter of our city's mayor. She was the kind of person who gained your trust automatically. But when it came time to accept responsibility for her actions, she let others take the fall. It was disappointing.

After the suspension, I returned to school, but it was never the same. The teachers now labeled me as one of the "troublemakers." Suddenly I couldn't open my backpack to get a pencil without being yelled at. I found myself called out for the slightest transgressions; things I would never have been admonished over before. I tried to get back in the good graces of my teachers, but it felt like I couldn't win. Eventually I gave up. Once judgment was cast, they never let me back in. This experience gave me a lot of compassion for the kids who were "constantly in trouble." Sure, they fooled around and got in trouble sometimes. But when it really mattered, they took responsibility for their actions, never pointing the finger at anyone else. Whatever their other shortcomings, I respected that they took ownership.

I wonder how often the innocent are unjustly punished.

I wonder if Jessica followed in her father's footsteps and became a politician.

I wonder how many kids get some label and are never able to shake it.

I wonder if one day we'll learn to truly forgive and allow people to return to their former state of grace.

I wonder how many people are reading this to find out how to remove gummi bears from their ceilings.

Chapter 25

Great Coach

I played soccer for nine and a half years, and one season I ended up on the second-worst team in the league. We were bad. But as bad as we were, there was one team doing even worse. On the day we were set to play them, my coach started me as a forward instead of my usual spot as a goalie. I was excited to get to play offense, and just five minutes into the game, we made a drive toward a loose ball that was in front of the opposing team's goal. Their goalie was running to intercept it, but as he dove, I kicked a low grounder that went right under him. It was my first goal of the season, and being a goalie, it was also my only goal of the season. After that we were up one point, so Coach moved me back to my normal position. Within minutes, our guys scored two more goals, and by the end of the third quarter, we were winning with a score of seven to zero. By then I was feeling bad for the other team. Rumor was that their coach had dropped out mid-season, and with no one to replace him, one of the kids' moms had taken over the job. I remember her standing on the side of the field yelling instructions and doing her best, but it was disorganized, and the kids' morale just wasn't there.

In frustration, one of their defenders stopped the ball with his hands. The referee blew the whistle and we were awarded a penalty kick. Instantly, ten hands shot up, including mine. We all wanted Coach to pick us to make the penalty shot. But Coach just stood at the sidelines in silence as we all serenaded him with, "Coach, Coach!" When we eventually quieted down, he raised both of his hands to the sides of his mouth to make a mini megaphone. Then, in a loud clear voice he shouted, "Brian!" All our jaws dropped in shock. Brian? I looked over at Brian and his expression was just as surprised as ours. He was the only kid who hadn't raised his hand wanting to take the shot, probably because he never learned to kick the ball right. He was always using his toe, which sent the ball flying off in unpredictable directions. Brian stood frozen in place as we all stared at him.

From the sideline, Coach shouted again, "Brian!" With the air of a man condemned to the gallows, Brian trudged his sumo-shaped body to the penalty line. The referee crouched and nimbly set the ball in place, his spritely movements in juxtaposition to the child giant. All the other players took their positions, ready to move in case the ball was deflected, giving us a second shot at it. Brian stood deeply into his heels, making his already pigeoned toes look more pronounced. There was no setup. He didn't measure the distance or bend his knees in preparation. He just stood there for a few moments; thighs so thick they touched down to the knees. Then the referee blew his whistle, and Brian tipped forward like a redwood being felled for timber, first slow, but gaining momentum with every inch. His feet began a surprised scurry as if they'd been unaware of their involvement in this task. One step, two steps, his right foot made contact with the ball. I was all the way back in our goalie box, but I heard the leather and rubber groan from the force. The ball traveled upwards and to the right, and the goalie dove towards it. His fingers caught the edge of the ball, but the momentum was too great. The ball carried through only stopping when it hit the net. *GOOOOOAL!!!* All of our players raised their hands high in victory and converged as a mob around Brian. There was no victory lap. Brian didn't run around the field, take his shirt off or even raise his hands. But as our guys were laying their hands on him and literally jumping up and down in celebration, I saw something I had never seen before. Brian was smiling.

Brian had made the final goal of the only game we won all season. After that Brian showed up to every practice and game. He dedicated himself in every way he could and was a valued member of the team. More than once the story of his goal was told over pizza and pitchers of rootbeer. And whenever it was, Brian would sit there smiling.

I don't know if Coach knew all of this when he called for Brian to take the shot. But with that decision, he taught me one of the most valuable lessons of my life. If you have a chance to elevate someone, take it. They still have to make it happen. You can't take the shots for them. But if you can put someone in a position to make their play, do it.

Moments like this make life worth living.

Chapter 26

Subtle Probings of the Bully

O ne of the techniques many bullies use for selecting a target is the compliance test. They will ask you for some simple thing or favor: "Can I borrow a dollar?" "Will you bring me a soda?" "Can you put more paper in the office printer?" They usually say it very sweetly, and because it's such a small request, you feel like an ass to say no. So, you do the task, granting the favor, behaving exactly as any decent human being would. But now they know that you'll do things for them, and the cycle has begun. The next time, they will ask for a little more, and a little more, then more. Eventually they stop asking so nicely, and if you ever try to refuse, they'll blow up or sling guilt trips at you. They make you feel bad for standing up to them. This is the critical moment: if you give in to their pressure, if you placate them, if you do not stand up for yourself, they've got you. And they will not let go without a fight.

I learned this lesson at a young age. One of my brothers asked me in his best I'M SO EXHAUSTED voice, "Billy, can you get me a glass of milk?" It sounded innocent, but something about the way he said it told me that he was acting tired just to get me to do it.

Very nicely I said, "I'm tired too. Can you get it yourself?"

His reaction was immediate. He threw the TV remote down on the sofa and shouted, "Fine, I'll get it myself, but don't you ever fuckin' ask me for anything!" Then, he stormed off to the kitchen.

I was shocked and confused by the severity of the outburst. Then it occurred to me. He wasn't mad that I didn't get the milk. He was mad that I didn't let him control me. Moments later, he came back from the kitchen and threatened to pour the glass of milk over my head. I ran for the front door to try and get out of the house, but he was much bigger than me. He grabbed my arm and with all of his weight smashed me up against the wall. I remember feeling my feet dangling in the air above the floor. He continued shouting at me, but I don't remember what he said. As I struggled to breathe, I retreated into my own thoughts.

This is how bullies operate. When they don't get their way, they impose their will on others by force. This is an extreme example, and you shouldn't assume that anytime a person asks for a favor or help with something they are trying to manipulate you. In a healthy relationship it's normal to make requests of one another.

What I am saying is to watch for early signs of this type of bullying. Be careful that your kind nature is not misinterpreted as weakness. Bullies only understand power, so you must be on guard, ever ready to stand up for yourself. Yes, it feels uncomfortable, but if you give in at the beginning, often a few months down the road their abuse will have increased tenfold. It will be much harder to convince the bully that you're not a target if you've already been compliant with their requests early on.

Chapter 27

Pay the Tax

I didn't grow up in the best area. I'd heard our hometown was the crystal meth capital of the US at the time, but I didn't know if it was actually true. There was gang activity and drugs, and it didn't help that the middle of my street marked the border between the two cities. The houses on my side of the street were in town A, and the houses across the street were in town B. So, whenever something illegal happened on our block, the police would run into jurisdiction issues. Criminals knew this so they would come to our neighborhood to ply their trade, and they stayed busy.

On this day my best friend, Mike (who was black) and I were walking to the same store as I had been the time I had a gun pointed at me. We were a few hundred yards away from the railroad tracks when we spotted the beggars. They were a gang of black teenagers who always shook Mike down for money. He'd tell them that he didn't have anything on him, but they knew he was going to the store to play video games, so they would search him and take anything valuable. He took to carrying money in his sock because they'd never checked there.

Two of the beggars approached to perform one of these searches.

After they'd finished with Mike, the bigger of the two kids pointed at me and told his friend, "Now, search him."

I had $20 in my pocket, and I firmly said, "I don't have anything for you." The kid hesitated, then made a few threats, but eventually he left me alone. As we walked farther, more of them showed up, until it was six or seven of them against us. And judging by the way they circled up, I knew something was gonna go down. We continued on, ready for anything, but to my surprise, they let us pass. This was a first. They always came at us. I wondered if standing up for myself had worked. But just when I thought we were home free, I heard one of the bigger ones shout, "Hey white boy!" Mike and I looked back at their leader, and he motioned us over saying, "I wanna talk to you!"

I knew it wasn't going to be a friendly talk. They were going to fine me for not letting the first kid do his job. So I shook my head no and continued walking. The big one yelled again, "Hey, I said get your ass over here!"

We continued walking while simultaneously watching them over our shoulders. That's when I realized why they'd been circled up the way they were. One of the younger kids stepped forward with a rifle. The leader looked down at him and nodded. The kid brought the rifle to his shoulder and began to sight us in. Despite this, my impulse was to keep walking at our normal pace so as not to give them the satisfaction. Luckily Mike's reaction was to bolt for the railroad tracks, running for all he was worth. That triggered me to run as well, setting a speed record of my own. I heard a soft popping sound followed by a sting in the middle of my back, but I kept running. When we had finally made it across the tracks and were certain they weren't coming after us, I reached under my shirt to check my back. The stingy spot felt hot and wet, like sweat, but when I looked at my fingers, they were bright red. I exclaimed to Mike, "Did they shoot me?"

He lifted my shirt and said, "There's blood running down your back!"

Too concerned to be angry I asked, "How bad is it?"

He looked closer and found a hole about a quarter inch deep, and though it was bleeding, it wasn't life-threatening. He also found a hole in my shirt that lined up perfectly with the wound, so we knew for sure they'd shot me. There was also a second hole in my shirt just below the right armpit. This second hit passed through the gap between my arm and chest without hitting me. We decided they'd probably used an air rifle loaded with hunting pellets. Realizing that our lives had not been in real danger felt a little better, but as we walked, I got madder and madder. By the time I got home two hours later, after going the long way home instead of cutting across the tracks like we usually did, my thoughts had turned to vengeance.

I grabbed a mini baseball bat, the little souvenir ones a third the size of a regular bat. Then I loaded it into my school backpack, careful to leave a small part of the handle sticking out between the two zippers so I could easily reach back and deploy it without taking off the backpack. I walked back out to the street and went looking for them. Angry as I was, I'd cooled off enough that the little voice of reason started whispering to me, saying it wasn't worth it. I knew I was only going to get myself in more trouble, but I doggedly kept on. When I got there, not one of them was out, which was unusual. They were always out, making sure everyone paid their taxes, but this was the only time I'd ever seen that street deserted. Maybe they scattered after shooting me, figuring it would be best to lay low. Or maybe the universe was saving me from getting into the kind of trouble my brother and I had gotten into just months before when the other kids pointed guns at us. Either way, I'm glad nothing happened. Finding them would only have worsened the situation. Injuries, retaliation, making enemies, getting arrested, all of those things lay down a path I didn't want to go down. Turning for home, I swore to myself that I wouldn't let anger or petty desire for vengeance cloud my vision in the future. From then on, if something went down, I decided to set my feelings aside and operate from a place of logic and reason.

Chapter 28

The Pot Boiled Over

My mom raised me to be kind and not to start trouble. But all kids aren't raised this way. Some children are taught that might makes right, and they apply this philosophy at school. One day in eighth grade, a kid who picked on me all the time started up. Pushing and hitting me, he tried to take my backpack. I resisted but didn't fight back. My strategy was to be kind in the hopes of being treated kindly in return. "Do unto others as you would have them do unto you," and "Turn the other cheek," the typical tropes good parents teach their kids. But these techniques were useless when dealing with a playground bully. The bully wouldn't let up, hitting me repeatedly and calling me names. Still, I refused to engage. I didn't want to fight. But then he said, "Fuck your mother!"

Time stopped.

When he said that, he couldn't have known the effect it would have. He couldn't have known how many nights she sat next to my hospital bed when I was sick. How many times the nurses tried to tell her visiting hours were over, only to have the words die on their lips. How many times she had dropped everything to rush me to the emer-

87

gency room only to wait and see if this would be the time they couldn't fix me. He didn't know what she'd endured. Or that despite the many cases of abuse she'd weathered, she'd still come out the other side full of love for God and the world. Heck, if she'd been standing right there she'd have told me to forgive him. But she wasn't standing right there. And though there was a lot I'd put up with, insults to her honor wasn't on the list.

A deathly calm washed across me, a calm worse than anger. Anger is hot, and erratic, but this, this destroys worlds.

I turned to face him, something I typically avoided for fear of egging him on. Our eyes met. I watched him see the change. His over-confident demeanor vanished, and the sneering lip softened. I began to move towards him with a singularity of purpose. He melted before me, backing away, hands raised placatingly as he shouted, "No, don't! Please!" Then he turned and ran as fast as he could.

I stopped and watched as he disappeared behind the school's administrative building, shocked at this sudden turn of events. I didn't give chase, and time returned to normal. As the adrenaline burned off, a soft shaking materialized throughout my body. "What a coward," I thought. "He'd been asking for this for weeks, and now when I'm ready to give it, he runs away."

The school bell rang, reminding me to get to class, so I turned to make my way. As I walked, I thought about the preceding weeks. How he'd started small, blocking my locker and refusing to move. I'd tried to ignore him. But the more I ignored him, the more abusive he had become. And still, I'd refused to stand up for myself. But the second he verbally attacked my mom, I leapt to her defense. I was ready to stand up for her honor with no hesitation, when just moments earlier, I'd been unwilling to defend my own. I considered this, trying to figure out why I'd responded so differently. The answer took form in my thoughts.

"I don't love myself enough to do for me, what I'll unhesitatingly do for her."

Wow, there it was.

I learned a valuable lesson in self-love that day. And I vowed right there in front of the math building to never again allow myself to be treated in a way I wouldn't allow my mother to be treated. I'd also learned that though there is a time for forgiveness and the turning of cheeks, there's also a time to say, I don't deserve to be abused, and I won't abide it.

Chapter 29

The Last Time

When my dad was a kid, his father whipped him every night for, "Everything you did today that I don't know about," with further tortures ready in case additional wrongs were discovered.

His mother wasn't much better. One time my dad and his sister were playing in the street in front of their home. Suddenly an out-of-control car came flying down the road. Behind the wheel of the car was their only neighbor, "Old Man Jack" struggling at the wheel. My dad ran to one side of the road, while his sister ran to the other. But then his sister yelled to him, "No, this way!" So, he ran back across the road so he could be on the same side she was, but there wasn't enough time. Old Man Jack's car smashed into him, literally tearing him out of his shoes and bouncing him down the road like a ragdoll. Battered and bleeding, he hobbled home, tears streaming freely down his young face. But when his mother came to the front door to see what all the commotion was, her first words were, "Where are your shoes? Go get your shoes!" So, my dad drug himself back up to the road to retrieve his shoes. They were in the exact spot in the road where he'd been hit. The impact literally tore his feet out of the shoes and both heels were split down the middle. When he returned to the house with damaged shoes, his mother blew up and gave him a beating. Then she made him sit in a chair and watch as she hand-sewed the torn heels back together.

These are just a few examples of the things he had to endure. And I think he grew to be a remarkably well-adjusted adult despite all that. He worked hard, and he was as good a dad as he knew how to be. But anyone who is a victim of abuse is certain to carry some dysfunction with them into their adult life.

When I was seven years old, my dad took me to a flea market. One of the vendors was selling calendars, so I asked my dad if I could get one. They were five dollars and I promised to reimburse the money as soon as we got home. He told me no, but before we left the vendor, he purchased two copies of the calendar I'd wanted. I thought he had changed his mind and purchased one for me after all. I mean, why get two of the exact same one if you're keeping them for yourself? If you're going to put one in the office, and one in the workshop, wouldn't you get different ones?

So, when we got home later that day, I got my five dollars, went to the garage, and exchanged the money for one of the calendars just like I'd promised to do. A little while later, I was playing in the driveway and my dad came marching angrily towards me. As he came close, he hit me. I remember because it was the hardest he had ever hit me. Then, grabbing my shoulders, he shook me, "You don't do that. I don't care about the money. You don't ever do that!" Then he pushed me away.

Despite moments like this, I never thought of my dad as being abusive. It was just normal, and I figured many others had it worse than me, so I didn't think much of it. But as I entered my teen years, he started getting physical more frequently.

When I was 13 or 14 years old, we were standing in the kitchen, and he got angry. He hit me in the shoulder so hard I felt my teeth rattle. Without thinking, I turned and hit him back, which shocked us both. I'd never fought back before. My retaliation infuriated him all the more. He hauled back and hit me so hard I fell into the dining room table. Undeterred, I pulled myself back up, marched across the kitchen, and hit him right back.

We stood there glaring at each other. He visibly shook with anger, then growled menacingly, "You don't know what you're making me do." I could feel he was right at the edge of exploding. But he managed to control his temper and finally turned away.

It was the first time I'd ever, "won" one of these exchanges.

That day opened a new chapter, and for the next few months anytime he hit me, I hit him back. Always in the same place he had hit me, and always with the same intensity. For a few months, that was our new normal. But then one day he came home in a particularly bad mood. After we'd exchanged a few cursory punches, he exploded and came at me. I ran for my room, just trying to get out of his way, but he followed me. As I closed the bedroom door he slammed into the other side, bursting through. What happened next is a blur of fear and fury, but my mom describes it as "And that's when you threw him across the room."

The next thing I do remember is seeing my dad sprawled back on the bed. His right hand raised in front of him defensively shouting, "What's the matter with you?"

As I stood there looking into his eyes, I saw something I'd never seen before, fear.

At that moment my dad ceased to be the otherworldly superhero I'd always envisioned him to be. For the first time, he was human. He must have felt the change too, because that was the last time he ever hit me.

It's taken a long time to try and puzzle out why this story has felt so important to tell. Is it about standing up for yourself? Or how we idolize our parents? Is it a cautionary tale about not passing on dysfunction and trauma to our children? Maybe it's a little of them all, but there's one more that's much less obvious.

When I finally reached my breaking point and started fighting back, I was not retaliating because of one punch. I was retaliating for hundreds of punches; punches that had accumulated over time. From him, from my brothers, from the school bullies, all of it had built up into this one moment. I didn't want to fight with my dad, but that's what it took for him to hear me. It's what it took before he realized I wasn't going to accept any bullying anymore. And the craziest thing about it, I don't think he'd ever realized before that he was even doing something wrong. I think he was trying his best to be a good dad and a good disciplinarian. Or he was just doing what his parents had done with him.

Since then, I've often asked people, "Do you think your parents did things right for you when you were growing up?"

And so often the answer is something to the effect of, "Oh no, they didn't get it. They tried this or that, but it never worked. I'd sneak out and do things I wasn't supposed to."

But then these same people who'd claimed that the techniques their parents had used didn't work, use the same techniques on their own kids. It makes no sense to me. Why would you parent in the same ways that hadn't worked for you? Are we doomed to repeat the teachings of our parents, both the good and the bad? I'm in no way suggesting that parenting is easy. I'm convinced enough of its difficulty that I chose not to have any kids of my own. But I can't help but wonder why we do the things our parents did, even when they don't make sense. I've tried to identify and change those things in myself, taking the best of their teachings to heart while leaving behind the things that didn't work.

Your parents did the best job they knew how to do. Mine did too. Now we have to take what worked, discard what didn't, and fill in the gaps that keep us from getting where we want to go. It's not easy, but the answer to every problem is out there if you're willing to do the work of finding it.

Chapter 30

Watch Out for Life's Trailers

I was riding with my brother in his car when I saw two teenage boys walking on the sidewalk. As they approached the busy intersection, the green light turned yellow. They were still twenty yards from the corner, but not wanting to miss the opportunity to cross, they both took off running.

What they did not see was a big white truck also trying to make the light.

Right as the two boys entered the intersection, the white truck turned in front of them. I watched in dread, unable to intervene. One of the boys saw the vehicle and managed to stop short with just centimeters to spare, but the other had so much momentum he crashed into the side of the passing cab. I saw his hands slap against the fender which helped slow him down. They both raised their hands in surprise and fury, then one of them flipped the driver off.

That should have been the end of it, and normally it would have been. But there was one more danger the boys hadn't anticipated. The truck was owned by a landscaping company and was pulling a long trailer filled with lawnmowers and yard tools. The boys failed to see the trailer as it carved a tighter path around the turn than the truck itself had.

Mercilessly the right rear wheels of the trailer mowed down the boy who'd run into the side of the truck, bouncing wildly as he went under its wheels.

I said to my brother, "You have to turn around. I just saw a kid get hit!"

My brother shook his head and said, "Oh no, I can't. I don't do well with that stuff."

Looking at him I said, "You have to go back. I saw everything."

Reluctantly he turned into the next driveway and swung back around.

As soon as we were close enough, I jumped out of the car and ran to the scene. The boy who had been run over was lying on his back, moaning loudly as he rolled back and forth in agony. His white shirt was dirty with asphalt and grease stains, but for having been run over, he didn't look that bad. I continued the examination and discovered his left foot flopped over at a bizarre angle. It was facing the wrong way and halfway torn off. The now exposed ankle bone gleamed in a surreal pearly white. I'd never imagined bone could look so clean and fresh. Despite the severity, none of the arteries were damaged, and his bleeding was minimal. As I was taking all this in, the boy looked at me. His expression was like an unspoken question, "Who are you and why are you here?"

"You're going to be okay," I said reassuringly.

Seemingly satisfied with that, he laid back and resumed his rocking and agonized moaning.

His friend who'd only narrowly escaped the same fate took a knee right next to us. His eyes were glazed over in shock, and he kept repeating the same sentence over and over, "I'm so sorry dawg. I shouldn't have rushed you. I'm so sorry dawg."

The truck didn't stop, and I wondered if the driver even knew he'd hit someone.

Two police cars rolled up. They must have been close enough to see some of what had happened because one of them joined us while the other went after the truck.

I stayed out of the way while the professionals did their work. After the boy had been loaded into an ambulance, the officer who'd been first on the scene asked me what had happened, and I gave a statement.

After that, we left, and I never heard anything more about it. I always wondered if they were able to reattach the foot and what the boy's long-term prognosis was. Whatever the end results, I'm certain his life was forever changed that day.

It would be easy to say, "They shouldn't have rushed" or, "None of this would have happened if they'd been a little more patient." But maybe that's not the whole takeaway. Sometimes getting something done quickly is beneficial. So maybe it's better to say, "If only they'd remained vigilant to everything going on in their environment, this wouldn't have happened."

Watching this chain of events unfold reminded me to be proactive instead of reactive. Arguably they were, at least at first, being proactive when they ran for the light, which is good. However, they did not anticipate how the environmental change of the light turning yellow would affect other variables around them, like the truck. They only considered their own desire to make the light. If either of the boys had thought to look over their shoulder and double-check that it was still safe to cross (proactive) maybe the accident wouldn't have happened. When the boys entered the intersection and ran into the truck, that was the moment they became aware that they'd overlooked something. This caused them to become reactive, expressing anger at the driver for not seeing them.

If instead of using that short moment to express their anger, they'd instead re-evaluated the situation, might they have seen the trailer and managed to get out of the way in time? Maybe or maybe not. Sometimes accidents are unavoidable. Our mindset can reduce the danger of a situation, but nothing can ever fully insulate you.

I've considered this event and all that went wrong for a long time, and these are the biggest takeaways for me:

* Always stay aware of your surroundings.

* Getting angry is not always helpful, so don't allow yourself to get angry impulsively.

* Try to operate proactively; anticipate the ripples your actions and decisions will create, and adjust future behaviors based on past observations.

Chapter 31

So I Sprayed Him

I was standing in line at the bank when I felt something poke me in the butt. It wasn't an innocent, "Oh, I'm so sorry, then we all move on" kind of bump. This was a dead center, crack splitting, hole puckering, bull's eye. Startled, I jumped forward, turned 180 degrees in midair, and was ready to face this unknown threat. But all I saw was a married couple standing a comfortable distance behind me. They talked quietly amongst themselves, oblivious to my presence. Knowing I wasn't imagining things, I continued to scan the room, but nothing seemed out of order.

I turned forward again and something entered my peripheral. Looking straight down for the first time, I saw a young boy standing so close to my legs that we were almost touching. I took a decisive step back, then looked at him expectantly. But he didn't make eye contact. He just stood there frozen, head hung slightly. I looked up at the parents to see if they had noticed, but they were in their own world. I considered the situation for a moment, then decided it was just an accident. He was probably embarrassed, which made me feel bad for him. So, I quietly turned back around to continue waiting.

Around 15 seconds passed before the exact same thing

happened! I stepped forward again, but the boy stepped forward too, smushing his face firmly between my ass cheeks. I looked over my shoulder at the parents, incredulous that this was happening. I expected them to notice and step in, but they were clueless. I stood there a moment longer, contemplating what to do. I couldn't walk any farther forward without bumping into the person ahead of me. I was trapped. But just then, when I was the most lost as to how to handle this bizarre situation, the universe offered a solution. As I stood there, feeling the tip of his little nose pressed home, my intestines gurgled gently, filling my rectum with gas. The little imaginary devil that lived on my left shoulder whispered in my ear, "Locked and loaded, sir."

Being a believer at the time, I looked up slightly and silently asked the ceiling, "Is it a sin to fart in a kid's face?"

But God gave no response, just the unceasing pressure from my behind.

Then the devil on my left shoulder whispered again, "It's what he wants. Why else would he put his nose there?"

"Yeah. Why else?" I thought back.

Slowly reaching the point of no return, I realized there was no other way. So I sprayed him.

Point blank, the blast engulfed his little face. The rush of warm air flowed directly into his nostrils.

Instantly the nagging pressure on my backside disappeared, never to return. I didn't look back; I made no acknowledgment. There was no need. The balance had been restored in the universe.

There are so many potential lessons in this story. Don't go poking your nose into other people's business; respect people's physical space; and beware of instant karma. But my hope is slightly different. I hope that one day I come across a book like this one, a book about life's lessons, and when I crack it open, I hope to read this same story but from the kid's perspective. If that encounter inspires him to one day write a book of his own, I think that would be just perfect. Inspiring the next generation, one kid at a time.

Chapter 32

Carjacked

My brother had been wrestling with drug and alcohol addiction for some time. He even sold drugs at one point to support his own habit. This got him into trouble of varying degrees. One time he'd done something that led to a high-speed chase, and the guys in the other car were trying to kill him. He managed to get away, but fearing for his life, he called our mom for help. He swore he was ready to get his life cleaned up, and she agreed to give him one more chance. He'd already burned his bridges with most of the family. But she agreed to let him stay for one night on the condition he'd check into a drug and alcohol rehab center the next morning. Having no other choice, he agreed.

I don't remember how he traveled the two hours from where he was to the area we were living, but he arrived safely and slept on the couch that night. From the moment he got in, he was peaches and cream, acting like a perfect gentleman. But when dawn broke the next morning, he started hemming and hawing about checking into rehab. He told my mom he was getting better and could handle this on his own.

My mom is an eternal optimist and always the first to give people a second chance. But his behavior over the years had worn out even her bottomless reserves. "I'm sorry honey," she said. "You've got to go and get help."

His calm demeanor cracked immediately, and his all too familiar rage began to bubble up. But he choked it back and smiled at her appeasingly. "Alright, you tell me when it's time to go."

She answered, "It's time," and picked up her keys.

All the way down the mountain, he tried every trick of persuasion he could come up with. He promised, begged, shouted, and threatened. Then he apologized and cried. All in an attempt to wear her down, but she stood firm.

When we got to the bottom of the hill, we stopped for a red light. As we waited, he tried one last time in his most heartbreaking, woe-is-me voice, "Mom, please, don't make me do this!"

She sat stoically, "I'm sorry baby, I really am, but you have to get help."

"Fuck this!" He barked as he simultaneously reached over and pulled her keys out of the ignition. Opening his door, he jumped out and barreled around the back of the car to get to her door.

"Lock your door, Billy!" she shouted to me in the backseat. We both held our fingers on the locks to keep them down.

Jamming the key he'd just stolen into her door lock, he started twisting and pulling to get the door open. "God damn it mom, open the *fucking door!*"

"Ricky please," she begged, "Please, why are you doing this? Stop! Please stop!"

"*Open the Fucking Door!*" He started smashing the back of his fist against her window trying to break it.

I wasn't old enough to drive, but because we lived on the mountain, my mom thought it important that I have my own key to the car in case some emergency should arise. She'd given me that key only a few weeks before, and while he was busy at her window, I reached into my pocket to retrieve it.

Changing tactics, he pulled the key out and came back to my

door, doubtless thinking he might have better luck overpowering me. As he did, I held the lock down with one hand and gave the keys to my mom with the other.

Seeing what was happening through the window, and realizing he was losing control, he started pleading again, "Mom, I'm sorry! *No*, let me in!"

She started the car, and seeing that the light had turned green started to pull forward.

"Mom, wait! Please, *Mom, Wait!*" he shouted as he ran back around the back of the car. He almost made it to the front passenger side door, but by then we were picking up speed. Realizing he was going to be left behind, he grabbed onto the roof rack and swung himself onto the side of our Toyota Corolla station wagon. Looking out the passenger side window I could see his exposed belly pressed against the glass. On it, a giant 14" scar ran from sternum to waistline, and at 2" wide, it had swallowed his belly button. Along its sides were countless little "centipede leg" looking scars from the nearly 200 staples the doctors had used to put him back together. We never got the whole story, but the rumor was that my brother had bullied a fellow soldier he'd been stationed with in the army. Then, for good measure, he'd fucked that man's girlfriend too. The next day, that soldier came looking for my brother, and when they met, he took out a knife and stabbed him in the stomach. My brother's liver was cut nearly in two, and had his barracks not lain adjacent to the base's hospital, he would have bled out. I mused on the fact that his recent car chase encounter, the reason he'd called my mom asking for help in the first place, was only the most recent time someone had tried to kill him. He certainly had a knack for pissing in people's Cheerios.

My mom turned wide, so the car was half in the shoulder and half on the road, but she continued on at 20mph.

She kept saying, "I have to stop! I have to stop!"

"No, keep driving." I said evenly.

"I have to stop!"

"No mom, you can't, just keep driving to the rehab center."

Her face scrunched up in a mix of emotions. She knew he would carjack us if she stopped, but it still took everything she had not to help her child.

A string of cars began to back up behind us. Partly because we're going slow, and partly out of curiosity. It's not every day you see a drug-crazed, 6'5", 260-pound man hanging off the side of a car screaming for his mom to stop.

This went on for another 15-30 seconds, him yelling and pleading all the way. Then he fell off. I watched as he tumbled end over end, kicking up a cloud of dust before disappearing off the edge of the embankment.

My mom's involuntary gasp translated into a physical slam on her brakes.

"Oh my god, he fell! I have to go back!"

"Mom, don't stop. You can't stop."

Tears of anguish sprung forth and ran down her cheeks. She was so torn, but she heard me, and she didn't stop.

As we drove on, I realized we had new problems. Assuming he was okay after the fall, he now had her keys. He had access to our house, her car, and anything else she had a key for. Fearful to go home, we stayed away all day and slept at a hotel that night.

The next morning my mom got someone from the drug and alcohol rehab center to go to our home with us. She was afraid my brother would take her down and steal the car if he was there, so she wanted an escort to help bring him in. A mile from our house, she pulled over and told me to get out. "If he's there, we'll take him. After you see us drive by, I want you to walk the rest of the home and wait for me. Or, if he's not there, I'll come back and pick you up. If we don't come back in the next 15 or 20 minutes, go to a neighbor's house and call for help."

Twenty minutes later I saw the car coming back, my mom, the escort, and my brother inside. I stood a little way back from the road so my brother wouldn't see me. Then after they'd passed, I walked home.

He did manage to get his life more on track after rehab, but the damage he'd done in those dark times was slow to heal. Still, I made an effort. Everyone deserves a chance to clean up.

A number of years later this same brother took my mom and I for $183k collectively in a real estate dealing. Her retirement nest egg vanished, and it left me with no reserves going into the 2008 real estate crash. I lost nearly everything when the bottom dropped out. After that, I was told by another family member that he'd also stolen money from our grandfather in his final years under the guise of "looking after him now that he has dementia," so I was done. I wish everyone the best in life, but our bridge wasn't burned, it was nuked.

Oh, one more gem. After he took our mom's last dollar, once she was totally broke with not a penny left to give, he never talked to her again. Today she's living off disability and a tiny social security pension. It's not what I wanted for her, and it's not how it should have been.

Chapter 33

The Murderer

I turned my truck onto the hillside road and the murderer came into view. His demeanor was relaxed, and why not? He has probably walked this way a hundred times. Why should today be any different? Why, indeed.

On the right side of the road was a tall cliff; the leftovers from when the narrow route was originally blasted out of the rock face. To the left is a tall block wall installed to prevent cars from slipping over the edge into the residents' backyards below. On this one-lane road, there were no curbs or sidewalks. It was so narrow it would be hard for a bicyclist to fit past a car if they were going in opposite directions. The top of the hill where the road opened back up is at least 80 yards ahead, and it was the only place he could escape. The universe created this moment just for me, and it was perfect. As I crept up the road, his pace quickened. Maybe it was his police training, or maybe it was some sixth sense telling him danger was close. But even at his best, even if he was still in his prime, he would never get to the top before I got him. My foot hovers over the accelerator, and I turn the steering wheel slightly to make sure he'll go directly under the tires. Then, just as I was about to unleash the tidal wave of pain and fury within me, a thought quietly whispered, "He's just an arthritic old dog. He did what he thought he was supposed to. He didn't intentionally cause pain and suffering."

Everything I had been thinking of doing held fast while I considered this.

Two days ago, this retired police dog had seen my cat sleeping in the driveway and attacked. He grabbed him, he shook, and he broke his back. The only reason Grey Kitty even survived the attack is that someone ran out and broke it up. Grey Kitty languished in a dirty old cardboard box for the next eight hours. And then, he died.

I didn't hear about it until after it was all over. They'd tried to reach me, but I didn't get there in time. I didn't get to scratch his chin or tell him what a good boy he'd been. He always loved the chin scritches. He'd get so lost in the euphoria that he'd drool all over my hand, but I didn't care. He was my lil' friend.

I looked again at the dirty black and brown fur shambling up the road. His hindquarters were stiffened and created a slight limp. I wondered how many criminals he had caught; how many kids were saved because of the drugs he had sniffed out; how many times he protected the life of his master or the life of another officer in their time of need.

I didn't know, but I was sure he had tried his very best to be a good boy.

I felt my foot relax, no longer thinking of pressing the gas. And, soon enough, we arrived at the top of the hill. The block wall ended, and he turned down the driveway that led to the safety of his home and the friendly people who'd adopted him after the police force could no longer use him. They must have known they'd only get to love him for a few years. They must have known those years would be tough, and they'd have to say goodbye before they were ready. But even knowing that they took him in any way.

Halfway down the driveway, he stopped and turned to look back at me. His dark eyes found mine and we held eye contact for a few moments. Somehow, I knew he was reading my thoughts, that he knew everything I'd been thinking. Then I heard his spirit whisper, "Thank you for letting me live. "

And, through my tears, I whispered back, "Thank you for teaching me to forgive."

He nodded his head ever so slightly, then turned and trotted away.

Chapter 34

Love Tap

I was in the drive-thru of McDonald's waiting for the car in front of me to finish ordering. Eventually, they pulled forward, and I rolled up to the intercom box. I waited until I heard the familiar rasp, "Can I take your order?"

"Yeah, gimme a..." but I was cut off when I felt the car wiggle and emit a dull plastic like kind of sound.

"I'm sorry, what was your order?" the voice from the kiosk statically asked.

"Hold on, I think my car just got hit," I responded.

Putting it in park, I opened the door and walked back to take a look. Sure enough, the bumper of the car behind me was in contact with mine. Looking up I saw the elderly lady behind the wheel of an old, station wagon-type car. She made no apology and gave no indication that she even realized it happened. Looking at the bumper again I could see there was no real damage, and I'd barely even felt the impact. So, I looked back at her and waved my hand as if saying, "No big deal." Then I got back into my car and ordered my food.

Each time I moved forward I watched her in the rearview mirror to see if she'd get too close or hit me again, but she didn't. Other than

108

the fact that she'd bumped me, nothing else was out of the ordinary. A few minutes later I got to the window, and they asked me to wait in one of the spots they like to send you to when your order is going to take a little longer. I moved to the spot and then watched the lady who'd been behind me pull up and collect her food. Once she had her items, she accelerated towards the exit of the parking lot and without stopping, pulled straight out onto the busy street. Before she'd even cleared the driveway a big dually-style truck smashed straight into her driver's side doorpost. The impact pushed her car sideways three to four car lengths, and as the whole mess came to rest, she slumped limply into the passenger's seat.

I knew it was bad and undid my seatbelt so I could jump out and help, but a fire truck that was coming from the opposite direction flipped on its lights and pulled straight into the fray. Seconds later, a dazed McDonald's employee pushed a bag through my window, her eyes glued on the scene unfolding in the street. I accepted the bag and she walked away.

I figured more emergency vehicles would arrive soon, so I vacated the area. As I drove away, I was struck by the fact that I'd had the opportunity to possibly stop this. When she'd hit me, she seemed out of it. Deep down I knew that something was off, but I didn't listen to my instincts. I did what I thought was the nice thing, which was to give this old lady a break and not make a big deal out of a damage-less tap on my bumper. But then something ten times worse happened. It's been decades since, and I still think about it. I still wrestle with what I could have done differently. It's one of the countless lessons I carry with me each day. If something feels off, it probably is. Always trust your instincts.

Chapter 35

Meeting New People

I was 20 years old and hoping to make friends in a new area, so I visited a church that was down the street from my apartment. Walking in, I grabbed an open seat and settled in next to a small family. I waited to see if they would greet me, but they didn't. In fact, they ignored me completely. The father was closest to me, but his body language was very closed off, so I didn't try to initiate any conversation. A few minutes later the service started and not one person had tried to talk with me or welcome me to the space.

My impression was that it wasn't a very friendly place.

Then, partway through the service, the pastor asked the assembly, "Is anyone visiting us for the first time?"

I raised my hand, hoping someone would notice that I was new and come break the ice with me later. That's when I noticed the family next to me had all raised their hands as well. They were also visiting for the first time.

These people who I'd thought were unfriendly regulars, were actually just as new and unfamiliar with the place as I was. They hadn't welcomed me into the space because they didn't feel it was their space to offer.

That left me wondering, maybe they'd been thinking some of the same things about me that I had of them. Maybe they thought I was the regular who'd been unfriendly. Here they were visiting a new church and the person who sat down next to them didn't even say, "Hi."

I considered this for the rest of the service, and when things wrapped up, I made a point to warmly welcome this family to the church. And as is so often the case when we give people a chance, they were very nice. We had a pleasant conversation, and they were happy to interact once I'd taken the initiative to open up.

I've carried that lesson with me ever since. Regardless of whether you feel at home in a space or not, we can still be welcoming to our fellow human beings anywhere, anytime. So, the next time you're meeting new people, try pushing yourself to make the first move. Even if you just say, "Hi." I think you'll be surprised by the results.

Chapter 36

Surfing a 21' Day

I pressed the pen against the paper and wrote, "If I don't come back, tell my mom I was doing what I love." I carefully tore the page out of my notebook and slid it under the pillow.

For three days, the surf off the coast of San Diego had been building, and on that day its forecast was to peak with 21-foot sets. These were the biggest waves I had ever tried to ride. Two days prior it was 16 feet, and I broke my favorite surfboard that day. The day before, it had built to 19 feet, and I broke my second favorite board. On this day, I would be taking out my third string ride, an off brand, 7'4", hybrid tri-fin that was extra floaty. I knew it would be tough to push this thing deep and get under the breakers. It was definitely not my preferred board for a day like that. I put on my rash guard shirt and 3-2 O'Neill wetsuit, but I only pulled the wetsuit up to my waist at first. There was no need to prematurely agitate my already badly chaffed neck.

My Freestyle Shark watch beeped right at 8 am; it was go time. My roommate and I picked up our boards and headed out to the car. We only lived a mile from the beach, but our favorite break was "Grandview," which was a little further up the coast. We arrived at the parking lot and pulled out our gear. This was normally where we giddily began to race down the winding staircase that transitioned from the top of the sea cliff to the sandy shore below. But the energy was different. We made our way quietly down the stairs, stopping at each overlook to observe the incoming swells. They were huge. We could hear the concussive crash echoing off the cliffs as each one broke. All I could think was, "And those aren't even the set waves." Finally, our feet hit the sand and we made our way out towards the water's edge.

I set my board down and scrubbed a fresh coat of Sticky Bumps surf wax onto it so my feet would find traction. I velcroed my leash to my right ankle, careful that the emergency tab was easily located in case I needed to cut myself loose. And of course, I pulled on the rest of the wetsuit. I reached behind myself to grab the long cord that was attached to the zipper of the wetsuit, so I could glide it up my back. Then, I strapped the neck velcro in place. Even with the rash guard to protect me, it was really painful. But that was normal when you were surfing as much as I was. My wetsuit rash never really healed between sessions. Like a bad case of Fiddler's neck, it just became the new normal.

I picked up my board and stared out at the water, waiting. Watching everything. What was the ocean saying today? Where was it the weakest and most powerful? Were there riptides? Any exposed rocks? Was the wind favorable? What was the fastest route through the inside waves? I looked to the shore and found a landmark to orient myself against. I chose a boarded-up lifeguard stand. It was off season, so we would be on our own. I had been surfing 3-5 days a week for two years, and I was in the best shape of my life. Still, this wasn't a normal day, and I couldn't help but note that we were the only ones out.

Not even one other surfer was there; an unheard of scenario in the crowded San Diego scene.

We turned towards the water and began to jog out. The water hit my ankles, then calves, and finally knees. Then the jog turned into a high knee shuffle as we covered as much distance as possible before plunging into the icy water. Grandview had an inner and an outer break. First the waves broke on the outside, and then a second time on the inside. But by then the wave usually lost a lot of its power. But on that day even the inside waves were brutal. For every ten feet of forward progress we made, the next wave knocked us back eight. We struggled for 20 minutes just to make it past the inside breakers. Then we took a moment to "rest" between the inner and outer sections. But it wasn't very refreshing because every 20-30 seconds we were pummeled by seven-foot-tall walls of whitewater, remnants of the outer break finding their way in. The waves were so big they trapped an unnaturally high level of air in them, which literally reduced the density of the water. I marveled at the way my paddle strokes passed through the water with unusual ease. We waited for a break in the sets, but it didn't come. So, we charged forward anyway, duck diving as best we could. Our familiarity with this location helped a little, but we were still tossed mercilessly. Eventually we made it past the outside break.

We had been paddling hard for 45 minutes. My friend and I both collapsed on our boards, breathing hard and trying to recover. I turned my head and looked towards the shore. In the hundreds of times I had surfed there, I had never been that far away from the land. The lifeguard stand I chose as a landmark wasn't even visible except when a swell floated me up high enough to briefly spy it. I turned my head towards the horizon, looking out at the open sea. When I was in this position, if I kept my focus, I could often see the most minute hints of a bump in the surface. This bump would race towards the shore and when it hit the underwater sea walls, it would well up to create the amazing surf California is famous for. I had always had a knack for spotting these bumps, and to my dismay, I spotted one that day. I shouted "Hup" to my friend and began to paddle hard straight out to sea.

If you can get to a wave before it breaks it will pass harmlessly beneath you. That is ideal. If you paddle towards it and it breaks ahead of you, it will begin to lose power and you duck dive under it. That is less ideal. If you paddle towards it and it breaks right on top of you, well, prepare for a pounding you won't soon forget. This is the worst-case scenario.

We were hoping to get to it before it broke. I paddled and paddled, making good time since the water on the outside was smoother. But as I watched the bump begin to form up, I felt my stomach drop. Omg! This wave was so big, it was going to break on an outer shelf we never even knew existed. I paddled harder than ever, but the wave welled up ominously. I realized there was no way we were going to beat this one. I stopped paddling and my board slowed in the water. I looked over at my friend who was still charging for the outside. He looked at me with an expression that screamed "Why aren't you paddling?" In response, I just shook my head from side to side. He looked out at the wave again and came to the same conclusion I had. He also stopped paddling.

We looked at each other one last time, an unspoken understanding passing between us. Then, in unison, we began to paddle away from each other. Not towards the wave, not towards the shore, just apart.

When a wave annihilates you, all control is lost. Your board can slam against you and leashes become entangled. During one of our surfing sessions, a friend had his lower lip split in half when one of his fins hit him in the face. So as a safety measure, we were making space, ensuring our own out of control boards and bodies would not place a friend in even more danger. Once we'd created sufficient distance, I gently slipped off my board. Conserving energy, I began to breathe slowly and deeply. The objective was to get in three deep wonderful breaths before I got hit. And if possible, pack extra air in on the last one. It was a free diving technique that helped a lot when I planned to be underwater for a long time. The wave was welling up, bigger, and bigger. I was hoping more than I'd ever hoped for anything that the wave would break before it got to me, losing a little of its power. Finally, the face became so steep it couldn't help but tube over. Two stories of water shattered the quiet as tons of water came down. The white water ricocheted 30 feet or more back up into the air! Awesome is a word much overused, but seeing this wave was awesome.

I flipped my board upside down and pushed it towards the shore. Then taking my final breath, I upended my feet and dove as deeply as I could go. I paddled until I could feel the board pulling firmly against my ankle leash. Then, I paddled even more to drag the board down after me into the depths. The deeper I went the more easily the wave could pass above me, at least that was the hope. With my right hand, I pinched my nose closed and held my wrist against my lips, squeezing hard. But the rest of my body relaxed. "Don't struggle. Don't panic. It's a waste of oxygen," is what I kept telling myself. Then I felt the water pressure change dramatically. The wave was above me, and beautifully it passed with relative ease. For half a moment I thought, "Maybe I'm gonna get off easy," but then the wave picked up my board. I felt a violent tug at my right ankle and was dragged upwards straight into the heart of the wave. My eyes were closed, but the darkness turned to light as the wave brought me all the way to the top. I knew what was coming. In surfing we call it, "Going over the falls." It's where the wave brings you over the top of the barrel and slams you out in front of itself, straight back into the most powerful part of the trough. The place you least want to be. The upward sensation began to change into a feeling of falling. I was riding the wave of my dreams, just not in the way I would have liked. The force, as I crashed back down, drove me so deep it got dark again. My ears screamed from the pressure. I tried to equalize them, but I couldn't. I can only describe it as what it must feel like to get hit by a bus, except it's malleable, so you have all the forces without the bludgeoning damage.

I felt the power begin to lessen, so I pushed my arms out wide, creating a sea brake with my body. I was trying to extricate myself from the waves' grip. But the wave had other plans. My board was still in its grip. I felt the familiar pull at my ankle and the upward sensation. "What? I'm going over the falls again!" Before I could finish this thought, I was ripped back towards the surface. I plugged my nose and mouth even harder as the process repeated. I went with everything as it happened, deeply relaxed in watery meditation but aware that I wouldn't have enough breath to go over the falls a third time. Once again, my ears began to scream from the pressure, bringing me out of my reverie. I begged, "Please, let me go," as I reached outward to make myself into a sea brake once again. And luckily, this time it worked. I felt the tension on my leash lessen, then release. It was still dark, but I had enough air in my lungs to be buoyant, so I waited to see which way my body would float. It was a great trick to make certain I was headed towards the surface. Unhurriedly, I swam upwards. There was always a chance that the moment my head popped up, another wave would be there ready to crash on top of me, so it was important to conserve air at all times. Finally, I came up, taking in a glorious breath of fresh air.

Air is so overlooked in our hierarchy of needs, but at that moment, I decided that breathing was most definitely my favorite thing to do. The water was white and foamy around me, and I again felt the lack of density in it as I struggled to tread water in the chop. Looking out towards the horizon, I was unsurprised to see the older sister of the wave that had just devastated me. These big set waves tended to come in threes on normal days, but during that time, the surf had been so big we'd become accustomed to sets of five! I realized that I might have to repeat this four more times before I was in the clear. I began to breathe deeply again in preparation. The second wave would be on me in a few seconds. Same strategy, dive deep, relax, go over the falls, don't panic, eventually find the surface. With the third wave, I did the same thing, but I could feel my oxygen reserves failing. Each holddown was taking a little bit more from me, leaving me less able to handle the next one. Popping again to the surface, I gasped for air. "Hold on, just two more," I thought. The fourth wave was the biggest yet. Like the first one, it took me over the falls twice. It pushed me so deep that I worried I would be smashed against the bottom. I reached for my leash and seriously considered cutting my board free. It was a catch-22. Unleashing the board meant I would be able to get under these monsters, but it also meant I would have nothing that floats, nothing to rest on top of to recover, and nothing to accelerate my journey back to the safety of the shore. I decided to hold out.

I reached the surface, and "Gassssppppppp!" Sweet air! I saw wave number five. It was even bigger, but it was the last one. I told myself I could do just one more. I barely remember this one. I folded in on myself and relaxed deeply even as my body was violently pummeled by water. I felt the fifth wave release me, and I rushed for the surface. I made it! I made it! Relief washed over me. I was already imagining lying on top of my board to catch my breath. As I planned my route back to shore, I stopped short. "Fuck! There's a sixth set wave coming straight for me!" I took a deep breath, dove, and faced another explosion. I relaxed deeper than ever, but the thought began to come, "This is how I die." I found the surface again. That was it. I had nothing left to give. I was spent. I could barely fight my head above the low-density bubble water to catch my breath.

Then I saw the seventh wave. I looked at it but felt nothing, no panic, no fear, only acceptance. I was too spent to even dive properly under it. I took my last breath, then allowed myself to sink feet first under the water. I didn't even consider unstrapping my board now. I was too tired to swim back to shore on my own anyway, and if I stayed attached to the board it would be easier for them to recover my body. All I remember from this wave was a feeling of curling myself into a ball, using my legs to help press my hand against my nose and mouth, sealing the water out and keeping every precious bubble of air in. Then it took me, dragging me through the water as if I was strapped to a power boat. There's nothing in the world like it. Nothing that can describe this utter powerlessness in the grasp of the sea.

An eternity seemed to pass, and I found myself at the surface again, gasping and coughing. Desperately I looked towards the horizon. But that was the end. There was no eighth wave coming for me. I looked around for my board but didn't see it. For a moment I feared that it might have been torn loose and taken by the wave, but then it appeared nearby. It had been pushed so far under that I'd beaten it to the surface.

I flipped the board right side up and with my last strength, I pulled myself up to lay on it. I had never felt so tired. But I had to stay alert. Another clean out set could roll in any minute. I looked for my friend but didn't see him anywhere. After a few moments I felt some strength return. All I wanted was to get back to the shore in one piece. I began to paddle towards land. This brought a new challenge. The break inside of my position was steadily throwing waves in the 15+ foot range. I was going on an hour straight of intense paddling and it was my third day in a row of being in big surf.

Normally I'd stand up and catch a ride in, but the idea of expending the energy necessary to get in and taking a chance of wiping out in the most powerful section of the wave felt overwhelming. I decided my best bet was to try and belly ride the whitewash in after the next big set came. I sat up on my board, just outside the second break, waiting for a good opportunity. As I sat there, I was struck by how thick the swells were. It was a literal mountain of water that floated me up ten to fifteen feet each time it passed underneath. And these were "the little ones."

I was grateful for the time to rest, but soon enough, another bump appeared on the horizon. As I waited, I realized when the outmost third break welled up, it stole the water from the inner two breaks. I could feel myself being pulled out to sea as this happened. I watched the outer break churn up its next 21-foot monster. It tubed over and crashed ominously. I gave thanks that I was no longer under that lip and no longer trapped in the impact zone.

Still, I had a massive wall of churning whitewater to contend with, and that was a serious problem. On a normal wave, you have a clean face to paddle down. It creates a natural downhill slope that allows you to add the power of the wave to your own propulsion.

Then at the right moment, you pop up to your feet and glide beautifully down the face. But whitewash doesn't have this downhill slope. The whitewash occurs when the wave has completely run itself over. All that's left is a turbulent, unrideable force of nature that wants nothing more than to destroy you. And worse, rather than pushing you forward, it sucks you backward into its maw.

I paddled towards the shore, letting the approaching wash use up as much of its energy as possible, but because it was pulling me back so strongly, I only managed to stay stationary. As it got closer, I realized there was no way I would be able to belly ride it in. This thing was going to run me over. Instinct took over. I stopped paddling and pushed the board out as far in front of me as possible. Holding onto the tail of the board with both hands, I took a huge breath, streamlined my body, and kicked my feet as hard as I could right as the 10-foot liquid avalanche enveloped me. I felt lifted up as the wave took control, bouncing every which way as I churned in the salty froth.

But the board being so buoyant saved the day. I held on as if my life depended on it and it dutifully kept me in the pocket, rocketing towards the shore. I was able to pull myself into a halfway respectable bodyboard posture, riding the maelstrom unsteadily. Normally when this happens you have to paddle and work to stay in the sweet spot, so the wave doesn't drop you. But this set wave had so much power, I just relaxed and rode steadily all the way to the shore. In time my skags hit bottom, dragging in the sand as the last of the wave turned into a harmless little shore break. I could see my friend walking towards me. He'd already been on shore for a few minutes having been lucky enough to get one nice ride before calling it quits.

I stood up and gathered myself. I undid the velcro on my leash, unzipped the wetsuit, and for the first time since I'd hit the water, I felt the familiar pain where the wetsuit always chaffed my neck. We took a moment to look back at the swells, listening to them crash. Then we both laughed. I guess when there are no words for something, a laugh is the best response.

Before that day I'd always been bigger than everything I'd put myself up against. This was the first time I wasn't strong enough or good enough to handle what I'd gotten myself into. In 21-foot surf, I'd finally found my edge. My hitherto aura of youthful invincibility was scrubbed away, and I walked back up the stairs humbler than the man who'd come down them.

Chapter 37

Robbed in Costa Rica

I was lying on my back under a big shade tree. The intermittent breeze brought the smell of fresh grass and waves of warm air from across the nearby soccer field. My girlfriend's keyboard was clicking busily as she worked on her homework. Its sound gently lulled me towards sleep. Everything was right. Even the itchy scratches from the Mexican blanket we were lying on felt good. This park was a hidden treasure in the busy San Jose landscape. I could see why she liked to work here. When we arrived, we had the place to ourselves. But then I heard the sound of a moped engine nearby. I figured it was someone on their lunch break who wanted to get a little sunshine. The engine puttered out and was soon replaced by a strange shuffling sound. It was familiar, but in my half-slumber, I couldn't place it. The sound got louder, and the tempo sped up. It was like the sound I heard when I played soccer as a kid. I would run through the grass and the longer strands would hit my shoes and make a distinct sound.

It kept getting louder until I knew what it was. Someone was running toward us! Snapping out of my reverie, I tried to sit up, but it was too late. I felt the broad butcher knife's blade press against my throat, and with his other hand, the attacker grabbed my shoulder. In one movement, he dropped to his knees forcing me back onto the blanket. In a thick Latin accent, he shouted, "Don't move!" I nodded my head gently as if to say, "Yeah, I know," and slowly raised my hands in capitulation. Out of the corner of my eye, I saw another man walk past. He was thinner than the man with the knife, tall too, but barely more than a boy. I made eye contact with him, and he quickly looked down at the ground. He wasn't proud of what he was doing. Despite this, he continued his work. He picked up my backpack and slung it over his shoulder. My laptop, camera, and most of my belongings were inside. Then he grabbed my girlfriend's backpack, but as he hefted it, she caught the shoulder strap with her hand and refused to let go. A violent tug of war ensued. He might have been thin, but he was standing up, which gave him leverage. Yanking hard, he pulled her forward from her seated position. She landed in an awkward sprawl on her belly. This brought her outreached hand within striking distance of the knife wielder. Fast as a cat, he slashed at her hand. Instinctively she pulled back, letting go of the backpack strap, and he returned the knife to my throat.

Having successfully collected most of our valuables, the thin guy ran back to the moped and started the engine. The man with the knife looked me in the eyes and pressed the blade hard against my throat repeating, "Don't move." Then, as quickly as they'd arrived, he leaped up, covered the distance, and jumped onto the back of the bike. I pulled my knees to my chest and exploded them outward to roll to my feet. But it was too late. They were already speeding away.

I had to hand it to them. It was a perfect crime, and it was partly my fault. The serenity of the place gave me a false sense of security, and I knew better than to let my guard down so completely. The two men reached the edge of the park where the grass turned to asphalt. Then they turned onto a side street. A plan began to form in my mind. Breaking into a full sprint I raced towards a different exit from the park, an exit that would allow me to head them off if they kept going in that same direction. I knew they were traveling towards a stoplight, and if they got caught at a red, I might have been able to intercept them. Yes, they still had the advantage. There were two of them and they had a knife. But I would be surprising them, and we would be in a public space where more people could see what was happening. My adrenaline surged. The initial fear turned to rage, and I covered several hundred yards in what felt like seconds. Bursting out on the main street, I saw that the traffic was indeed stopped at the red. I ran along the rows of cars looking for my adversaries, fully intending to do a flying sidekick at full sprint if I found them.

But they weren't there. I returned to the sidewalk when the light turned green but continued scanning the area. I knew every second lowered the chances of me catching them. A little side street I hadn't noticed before caught my eye. They saw us in the park, so maybe they lived nearby and pulled this stunt all the time. If so, that could be where they went. Jogging over, I slowly worked my way down the small street, looking for any sign of the bike or guys. Halfway down the block, a loud sharp sound came from directly behind me. It was a threatening sound, the sound of an attack. Instinct took over. In one motion, I pivoted 180° and launched a murderous left-footed roundhouse kick.

Everything moved in slow motion. My foot was a bullet, and the trigger had been pulled. I was just a bystander now. All I could do was watch to see what it destroyed. My foot flew straight towards the little black and brown Yorkie who'd stealthily snuck up behind me. His little expression dropped, and I realized he knew. He knew that this was the moment of his death. I heard his thoughts as clear as spoken words: "Why did I have to be so brave?" Instantly, I wanted to change everything, but it was too late. Reflexively he ducked his head low and closed his eyes so tightly his eyelids quivered. I heard his thoughts again: "This is gonna hurt so bad."

My foot flew straight through the space where his head had just been. The longest hairs on the top of his head brushed the sole of my foot, and the greasy fur along the side of his body rippled from the wind of my foot's passing. My leg continued upwards until it reached the end of its available travel, but it still didn't stop. My grounding foot was pulled from the earth, and I soared at least three more feet up off the ground before gravity overpowered adrenaline. As I touched back down, I saw the dog sprinting away. His tail was tucked so tight it made his back legs wobble funnily as he ran. He was looking back over his shoulder with a doggish, I'm so sorry grimace on his face.

Realizing my anger over the actions of the two criminals was nearly taken out on a little creature who had nothing to do with the crime, brought me back to earth. I felt foolish and regretted losing my head. Yes, the stuff they took was important. And yes, putting a knife to my throat wasn't the nicest thing they could have done. But the most important thing of all is that neither myself nor my girlfriend had been hurt. Stuff can be replaced, but life cannot.

Chapter 38

The Power Plant

"The Power Plant" is a well-known surf break in Carlsbad California, so it's usually crowded. But on one particular day, we had a whole section of the ocean to ourselves. Only a few scattered surfers were visible a little way down the coast.

I dropped into a beautiful 8-foot wave and popped up at just the right moment to carve a blade of water with my bottom turn. Then settling into the pocket, I transferred my weight back and forth from heel to toe, gliding the board gently up and down the face. I wasn't a hot dogger tearing it up. I just cruised and enjoyed the elegant dance with the sea. A few seconds later, the wave lost power and I cut cleanly out the back. Dropping to my belly, I began to paddle towards the outside, already imagining the next ride.

I duck dive a few incoming waves, slowly closing the distance between myself and my two friends. They were both beyond the break, waiting for "The Big-Katuna!" They were trying to catch the biggest wave of the day, so they let most of the swells pass by. I continued paddling but watched them closely, not wanting to miss the show if either of them got a nice one. Another biggish one rolled through, raising them upward. I could see their legs kicking lazily below in the crystal blue water. But right as they reached the highest point of the swell, a large shadow appeared in the water below them. It swam a little further before turning towards the surface and heading straight for my friends. I only saw it for a second, then the wave they were floating on broke, obscuring my view. It was unmistakable. There was a shark, the biggest I'd ever seen in open water. I stopped paddling, unsure what to do. Another swell rolled under them, and they floated into sight again. They looked relaxed. I could tell they didn't see it. I started to shout but the words died on my lips. They were too far away to hear me. And even if they could, my warning might make them panic. I didn't want to trigger an attack. I looked back towards the shore, and I was halfway between the sand and my friends.

I felt torn. Do I go to shore and wave my arms at them, hoping they see me and swim in? Or do I continue paddling out to warn them?

As I considered this, a medium sized wave welled up right in front of me. It was perfect in form. I could easily catch it and ride safely back to shore. It was a written invitation, so I turned for it, grateful for this opportunity to escape the danger. But at the last moment a thought came to me, "If one of them gets attacked, I will never forgive myself." The wave already had me, but I pushed myself backward. Instead of leaning forward to go with it, I dug my board's tail low in the water to act as a brake. The wave smacked into my back with a clap, then passed on, leaving me behind.

The action was unconscious and automatic. I spun around and began to paddle out. Suddenly my mind exploded with fear. I took deep breaths trying to stay calm. But as I paddled, each piece of kelp that touched my hand felt like an attack. Every shadow was an ominous omen. My momentum faltered because instinctively I had started arching my body, lifting as much of myself out of the water as possible. I was barely brushing the water's surface with my strokes for fear of giving the shark a bigger target. But then reason returned. I was in the shark's territory. It was an apex predator. There was absolutely nothing I could do to protect myself if it came, so why worry? I felt strength return to my arms, my legs relaxed back into the water, my board's rocker found its sweet spot and I dug my arms deeply and powerfully into the water. I felt a little better, but each time I dove under a wave, the fear returned. The thought of being attacked while underwater felt extra terrifying.

I continued on, and aside from my inner dialogue, the journey out to them was uneventful. I glided up next to them and my friend smiled and said, "You got a good one!"

"Thank you," I said. Then with a serious but calm tone I continued, "As I was paddling back out I saw a shark."

My friend's eyes widened, "Where? On the inside?"

"No," I said. "It was right underneath you guys, big one too. I'm guessing 13 feet, maybe bigger."

He looked around in the water suspiciously.

"Just relax," I said. "We'll all catch the next set in and meet up on shore."

He looked at me with an expression I couldn't decipher, then said, "You probably just saw a dolphin."

Losing a bit of my composure I shot back, "It was not a dolphin!"

He looked skeptical and raised one eyebrow.

I defended, "It was all by itself, not in a pod. It was bigger than any dolphin I've ever seen. Its tail swished side to side, not up and down like a dolphin's. Even the way its body moved when it turned towards the surface was shark-like!"

He smiled, then shook his head side to side dismissively.

Nearing desperation I said, "Listen, dolphins breathe air. Have you seen one dolphin spout since we've been here?"

He looked around again, then admitted that he hadn't seen any spouts. But he adamantly stood by his assertion that I'd seen a dolphin.

I wanted to argue. I wanted to tell him that I had dreamed of becoming a marine biologist since I was a kid. That sharks are my favorite animal. I've read every book and seen every documentary I could get my hands on. At Sea World, my parents regularly had to drag me out of the shark exhibit because I'd happily sit and watch them all day. What I'd seen had a shark's mannerisms. Its pectoral fins pointed stiffly downwards, and it had the bulbous lemon shaped body of a shark known to frequent these waters. And at that size, there was no doubt, it was a great white shark. But it was useless. He had made up his mind.

In resignation I said, "I'm going in on the next wave. I paddled out here to warn you of the danger, so my conscience is clear."

He smiled boyishly, oblivious to his mortality, "More waves for us," he said as he paddled off towards an approaching wave.

I paddled too, planning to catch the same wave back to shore, which I did. I rode it until I was as close to the shore as possible before jumping off, then waded the rest of the way in.

I gathered myself and sat on the beach without taking off my wetsuit. I kept my board leashed in case I had to go back out. I watched them catch a few more waves, while also keeping an eye out for the shark. In the back of my mind, I wondered what I'd do if one of them was attacked. I knew I'd have the impulse to help, but jeez, I warned them. Was I responsible for going back out there when I'd already put myself in danger once for their sake? I felt more torn than ever.

More time passed, but I didn't see the shark again. They continued to ride, enjoying the perfect uncrowded day. Eventually I even flirted with the idea of going back out myself but decided against it. I wandered up the walkway to the top of the cliff, watching the water as I went. Then I went to my truck and drove home. As I traveled down the road, I had a sinking feeling in my stomach and wondered if I'd see them both safely back at school on Monday.

No one got attacked that day. And despite what we see in movies, it's a fantastically rare occurrence. Still, when you know there's a shark in the area, it's wise to get out of the water, just as it's wise not to stand at the top of a mountain during a lightning storm.

This incident happened when I was a teenager, but it will always stay with me. If someone told me, "Look out, there's a huge lion outside," I'd respond, "Thanks, I think I'll stay inside then." I wouldn't argue with them and then wander outside! I still can't make sense of it.

Chapter 39

The Decimation

It's as impossible as trying to avoid rain drops while driving in the rain. I'm both awed by the beauty and destroyed by the fragility. They collected under the windshield wipers, only to be released like so much confetti whenever I activated the blades. The blue windshield fluid failed to penetrate the offal of their bodies now caked on the glass.

When I got into my truck that day, I didn't know what the wind, mountains, and forest had in store. I hadn't seen a single butterfly all day. But one mountain curve later, they were everywhere. Millions fluttered across the sunny meadow like a living blizzard that made the surrounding trees look dusted in snow. Each car that passed at 70 mph made a murderous contribution to the colorful carpet on the roadside. I slowed my vehicle to a crawl, but the wheels continued to churn the unlucky ones who'd landed on the road to paste. Ahead I saw a beige Lincoln town car parked on the other side of the road. An old man stood in front of it. The palms of his hands turned forward in a posture of helplessness, tears flowed freely down his cheeks. The butterflies lay around his feet like autumn leaves, stretching out like a river of white and gold. He wanted to do something, but what could be done? As I drove slowly past, he looked up and we made eye contact. I knew what he was thinking because I was thinking the same. Nothing was worth this.

If every human was given a cosmic quota of innocence and beauty they were allowed to destroy, each of us cashed our points in that day. An unwilling accomplice though I might have been, a piece of my heart was left on that road. It will be up there for as long as I live, dusted in the powder of a million shattered wings.

Chapter 40

Budman

I was on a first date and things were going well. But as we were driving to the restaurant, I noticed my truck's tank was almost empty. Pulling into the next gas station, I hopped out to fill up. As the pump chugged along, I noticed a long line of people inside the attached convenience store. It seemed odd since there were hardly any cars there. Looking closer I saw that every face in line was scowling. They were clearly irritated about something. Walking around the back of my truck, I was able to get a better view.

At the front of the line, I saw a middle-aged man with thinning hair. His clothes seemed normal enough, but disheveled, like he might be homeless. He seemed to be having some issues with his credit card. A few moments later, the automatic gas lever clicked off, so I walked over to put it back. As I was screwing my gas cap on, I noticed that the disheveled man was exiting the store. In his hands was a jumbo case of Budweiser, the type you might buy for a Super Bowl party. Getting back in my truck, I watched him perch the box precariously on the handlebars of his bicycle. An avid cyclist myself, I was impressed by the balance and control he had as he began to ride away. Starting the truck, I headed for the exit directly in front of me, but quickly realized it would be faster to exit on the other side of the station. So, I pulled a slow U-turn around the pumps and ended up driving in the same direction the cyclist had been going when he pulled away. As we approached the other exit, I realized the cyclist had disappeared. I was sure I didn't run him over. I would have felt the bump. I scanned his possible routes again, but he was nowhere to be seen. Half to myself but audibly I said, "Where'd he go?"

My date looked at me, "Where'd who go?"

A weird sensation rose in my gut, that telltale instinctual tightness when something is wrong. Putting the truck in park, I said to her, "I'm sure everything is fine, but keep the doors locked." Then I got out to look around. The sidewalk he was riding towards was wide open. If he'd gone that way, I would have been able to see him for at least three blocks. And if he had doubled back towards the other side of the station, I would have seen him when I was U-turning around the pumps. So, the only other direction he could have gone was behind the building itself. But if he was going that way, why get on the bike and ride? It was only a few steps away from where he was. He could have just walked his bike over there. It made no rational sense, but with no better clues, I wandered toward the back of the building to see if anything was out of the ordinary.

I reached the edge of the station's parking lot where there was a two-foot-tall concrete curb. It was high for a curb, and not a feature I'd normally pay any attention to, but it piqued my interest. As I got closer, I realized the curb was taller than normal because it wasn't a curb at all. It was the top of a five-foot-tall cinder block wall that surrounded the adjacent strip mall parking lot. The gas station was built on a mound, so it was two feet tall on our side. But on the strip mall side, it was a legitimate block wall. And with the difference in elevation, there was a notable drop. Stepping closer to the curb, I saw the cyclist down in the lower parking lot. He was lying face down across a concrete parking block, legs all tangled up in his bike. The only movement was from the dozen or so Budweiser cans rolling lazily outward. Calling down I asked, "Hey, man. You okay?" At the sound of my voice, he stirred and mumbled something unintelligible. Climbing down the wall, I knelt beside him and asked, "How can I help?" Seeming to get his bearings a little, he rolled to his side and started trying to untangle himself from the bike. I grabbed its frame and pulled to lift it off. As we did this, I noticed a nasty cut on his forehead. "Hey, you're bleeding," I said, pointing. Reaching his hand to the place I'd pointed, he wiped the blood and then looked at his hand in surprise. Standing up, I signaled to my date and shouted, "Can you bring me some napkins from the glovebox?"

She quickly grabbed some and brought them over. Then she collected the beer cans and put them back in the torn box as best she could.

"Do you want to go to the hospital?" I asked.

"Noooo, no, no," he answered in a drunken slur.

"Well, can I give you a ride somewhere?"

"Ohhhh, uh, sure, home."

Helping him up, I smelled the reek of alcohol.

"Ok buddy, let's go."

My date put his beer in the back of the truck, and I helped him crawl in beside it. Then I jogged back over to grab his bike and load it up as well. My date and I got back in the cab, and I opened up the little slide window in the back so I could talk to him.

"Which way?" I ask.

He looked around as if he was only just now realizing he was in the back of my truck. I waited patiently until he pointed off in the general direction he'd been heading when he'd first tried to ride away. "Makes sense," I replied and started driving that way. Within a block, he was lying down in the back of the truck, either passed out or sleeping. I shouted back to roust him, "Hey man, which way?"

Looking irritated, he sat up to get his bearings. He seemed lost and I began to wonder if we would even find his house. Eventually, he pointed again, so I turned left. We drove for another half mile, which gave the cool evening air a chance to work on him. He sat up and looked more engaged with our surroundings. He finally indicated to me to turn right, and we entered a neighborhood with dilapidated apartment buildings on both sides. About halfway up the block he said, "Here." I pulled over in front of the gated complex and started to ask him for the gate code, but then I saw that the pedestrian gate had been torn off its hinges and was now lying in the street where exiting vehicles had run over it repeatedly. I decided to park and take him in on foot. I told my date to keep the doors locked until I got back, and she nodded with an expression that said, "Yeah, duh."

Dropping the tailgate, I helped him out of the bed of the truck. He looked a bit more stable and managed to keep his feet on his own. I grabbed the bike in one hand and the broken case of beer in the other. "Alright, which one is yours?"

Without answering, he set off, and I followed behind him. We traveled past two buildings and then arrived at his apartment. It was a ground-level unit but for some reason, all the units had small staircases leading up to the door. We started up the seven-step staircase, but halfway up he lost balance and started to fall backward. My hands were full, so I braced and leaned forward, catching him against my left shoulder and chest. He teetered there for a moment, then restarted his upward shuffle. Reaching the top, he pulled out his keys and tried to open the door, but he couldn't find the right one in the darkness of the burned-out porch light. I offered to open it for him and without stepping aside or even looking at me, he held the keys out sideways. I took them and methodically tried each one. The third one, the one that lived next to a small keychain-style bottle opener, did the trick. Swinging the door wide, I motioned for him to enter first. He stepped into the darkness and turned to the right. I heard the rattle of empty aluminum cans rolling on the floor as he passed. Still wrestling with his beer and bike, I stepped in after him.

Once inside, the stench of a thousand dive bars assaulted my nostrils. I felt myself gagging and tried to hold my breath. Moving further into the dark space, the back wheel of the bike clipped a multitiered tower of empty beer cans near the front door and they noisily crashed to the floor. I started apologizing to him, but I saw him in the gloom crawling into a small bed in the corner. Flopping face down he passed out. Having adjusted to the darkness, I scanned the room, looking for a place to set the beer. There was a dining room table to my left, every inch of its flat surface dominated by vertical spires of empty Budweiser cans stacked four and five high. Straight ahead was the tiny kitchen, and every countertop had similar stacks of empty cans. Glancing at the refrigerator I saw that its top also had a mountain of aluminum. Every flat surface was stacked high with cans. Other than a few skinny walkways, every inch of the floor was buried in cans. There were even empty cans nestled around him in the bed. They held him delicately, swaddling him to sleep. Not seeing any other options, I set the case of beer on the floor in the middle of the pathway. Then I leaned his bike against the wall of cans between me and his bed. They avalanched under the weight until the bike settled against some unseen piece of furniture hidden beneath.

Budman slept through all of this, oblivious that I was even there. Feeling my duty fulfilled, I flipped the little locking mechanism on the inside of the doorknob and pulled the door tight behind me. When I got back to the truck, I noticed the tailgate was still down, so I closed it. A folded-up 20-dollar bill fell to the ground. I knew it belonged to Budman, but if I gave it back, he was just going to buy more beer. And besides, wasn't this the universe rewarding me for helping out? Still undecided, I asked my date what she thought we should do with the money. Without hesitation, she said, "You've earned that. Keep it!" I sure was tempted to do exactly that, but after thinking about it a second longer, I decided to return it. I had no right to judge how another person spent their money. Walking back to the now-familiar porch, I knocked but got no answer. I knocked again even stronger, but still, no answer. Kneeling down, I tried to push it under the door, but the jam wouldn't allow it. And there was no mailbox or doormat either. I considered putting it in the porch light, but the cobwebs and pile of dead bugs indicated it might just sit in there forever. At that point, I figured the universe was telling me to keep it, so I put it in my pocket. Later that night after my date and I had finished our dinner, I gave the $20 to our server as a tip. It seemed like the right thing to do.

This wasn't the first time I had encountered something like this. One time when I was a kid, we were driving down the street, and I saw a man lying on the side of the road. His legs were stiffened unnaturally, head hanging off the side of the sidewalk. I told my mom what I'd seen, and she turned around so we could investigate. As we approached on foot, I was pretty sure he was dead. There was no movement, and his whole body was perched like a stiff teeter board over his own disproportionately distended belly. My mom began to speak to him and after a minute he stirred. Rolling to his side, he slurred his words unintelligibly in our direction, intoxicated to the point that communication was impossible. Rolling to a seated position, the huge gash on his forehead began to douse his white t-shirt. He kept trying to wipe it away, but it only spread it. A concerned neighbor in a house close by called for an ambulance, so we stayed until it arrived. Once they started checking him out, we slowly slipped away. My mom could never turn away a stray. Be it an animal or a human in distress, she always stopped to help. I guess that rubbed off on me. I can't ignore the things that are happening around me, and that's why I helped the drunk guy get home after he fell off his bike. Maybe it won't change his life any. He might not even remember the incident, but I did what I knew was right to do, and that is enough.

Chapter 41

Knife Fight in Poland

"Mahhhhhwwwaaaahhhhhhh.   Mahwahhh.
MAHWAHHH!!! Maaaaaaaawahhh."

I had been lying in bed listening to this word repeated over and over since 6am. The hands on the old school clock above the bedroom door read 8:50am. I was losing my mind.

Turning to my girlfriend, I asked, "What does Mahwah mean?"

"It's his pet name for my mom," she replied in nearly accent free English.

"What does he want from her?"

"He wants her to clean up his vomit and piss." She looked down at the floor as she said this.

This was my third trip to Poland since we started dating. My girlfriend and I had dutifully made the trek to visit her family each year. I remembered how before our first trip she'd warned me about her father. As a young man, he was a soldier in the Polish military. After retiring from the service, he'd gone on to become a respected schoolteacher by day and alcohol infused tyrant by night. He'd regularly get drunk and then pass out on the living room sofa. During the night, his body would reach its breaking point and he would roll onto his side to vomit on the floor. He'd often follow this up by undoing his pants and urinating there as well. The oaken planks next to the sofa were twisted and bowed after years of this treatment.

When my girlfriend was a child, her father regularly beat her with a wooden table leg. When she matured and started dating, he'd initiated numerous altercations with her previous boyfriend. Another time he threw a knife at her mother and the blade had embedded into her leg. She'd been rushed to the hospital by a neighbor to get stitches. He had quite a reputation. Yet, despite that, he'd been a perfect gentleman during my first two visits. But this time he was showing his dark side.

"MAhhaaWWAhhh!!! MaHHHHwwaaa."

Through his cacophony we heard her mother's voice, soft but stern, ring out from the kitchen, "Wyczyść to sam!" My girlfriend translated, "Clean it yourself."

Her mother's resistance ignited an even more emphatic chant from the living room. "MMMMMaaAAHAHAHWAAHAHA-HA!!!! MAAAAA-WWAAAAAA-AAAAAAA!!!!"

A few minutes later I heard wheels rolling down the hallway. Her mother had prepared a mop and bucket for him. She delivered it to his room but made no effort to do the job for him, so he yelled at her in Polish. I couldn't understand the words but felt things escalating. My girlfriend got up and stood near our door. I could see she was afraid. I followed her, still believing this was a minor family tiff, but as soon as she opened the door enough for me to see, I realized the seriousness. Her mom was standing in the hallway pointing the mop at her father like a spear, keeping him back. He was standing in the living room holding a sheathed WWII bayonet, and they were screaming at each other. Without any hesitation, my girlfriend stepped across the hallway and got between them. Boldly she berated him in Polish, unconcerned by the deadly weapon in his hand. I stepped into the hallway and established myself, one step behind her and to the right. He was drunk enough to be unsteady, but sober enough to be dangerous. With his left hand, he grabbed the handle of the knife threateningly but didn't draw it. The energy in the space shifted, time slowed down, and everyone stopped shouting.

In my mind I was faced with a terrible choice: Do I attack him now while I still have the advantage, or do I wait until all other avenues have been exhausted and I have no choice? I pondered this for one millionth of a second before deciding that I would hold until I saw the glint of silver from the blade. Only then would I act. As I prepared, I felt the cotton rug beneath my feet slipping slightly. It wasn't rubberized on the back. If I moved quickly, it would slide, which would slow me. I casually reached up with my right hand to lean against the living room door frame. Strategically this would give me a solid element to launch from. I was struck by a thought: If this went sideways, I wasn't family. I would be the one who was going to get stabbed.

My girlfriend and her father glared stubbornly into each other's eyes, violence in the air. I leaned in over her shoulder, trying to make eye contact with him. I pleaded with every non-verbal cue at my command. I tried to energetically reach him since my words had no weight. But the alcohol had shut down his ability to reason, and the knife had made him bold. I saw it in his eyes. The decision was made. He tore the blade from its sheath. His left hand drew high, ready to bring the knife down in an overhand stab. My girlfriend jumped back as I leaped forward. Pivoting off my right foot and pulling hard against the door jam, I launched a ferocious left leg roundhouse kick. Despite the desperate nature of the situation, I didn't want to hurt him. I felt the sharpest part of my shinbone impact his belly under his right-side ribs. I didn't even follow through entirely with the kick, turning off the energy after the initial launch. But the strike was amply powerful. He flew across the room, landing heavily in his own puddle of dark yellow offal.

I spun around and started pushing my girlfriend and her mother towards the front door. "We have to get out," I shout. But it was pandemonium. Her mother was screaming in Polish, and my girl-friend was trying to tell me something, but I couldn't understand because she was also speaking Polish. Time was running out, and my back was exposed. I tried one last time to appeal to them, but they were unreachable. Just then I looked down and saw a small fabric carry-on bag sitting in the hallway. Not knowing what else to do, I picked it up and turned around. Lifting my canvas shield defensively, I maneuvered back toward the living room. Peeking in, I saw that he was still on the ground, knife in hand. "Drop it," I commanded. But he just stared at me with murder in his eyes. He lifted himself the rest of the way to his feet, but just as he caught his balance, I threw the empty piece of luggage straight into his face. He fell backward again and plopped into a seated position. He looked stunned for a moment, and then his puffy alcohol-addled face erupted. Blood poured freely from the creases between his eyes, above his left eyebrow, chin, and more. Wiping his face with his hand, he marveled at the blood, shocked to discover that he had been wounded. Under normal circumstances the fight would have been over. But he still had the knife, so he was still a threat. I took one step forward, preparing to close the distance and kick the blade out of his hand. But suddenly, I felt two hands grab me firmly from behind. It was my girlfriend. "This way!" she shouted. I allowed myself to be led back to her bedroom. As soon as we got inside, her mom closed and locked the door. For good measure she removed the old-fashioned barrel key from the lock. This all seemed like a good idea in the moment, but quickly I realized our mistake. We were on the third floor of an old Eastern Bloc apartment building. There was no fire escape and no way for us to get out except through the front door. We were trapped. A vision of rappelling down from the window on a rope made from bed linens flashed through my mind, but I dismissed it. Not only does that seem crazy, but it would also take time to construct. I didn't think her mom would be strong enough to do it safely anyway. We needed another solution.

I scanned the room with a new purpose, looking for anything that could be used as a weapon. But the pickings were slim. I settled on an eight foot long 2"x 2" stick they'd always meant to turn into a clothes rack, but never had. It was too long to be an effective staff, too blunt to be a good spear, and not heavy enough to be a bat. I decided it would be best as a spear and started looking for something to sharpen it with. But then I heard him outside in the hallway. He tried the door, but the lock held fast. I moved between the door and the two women in case he kicked it down, holding the blunt stick at the ready. Suddenly the skin-crawling sound of metal grinding on metal greeted my ears. I looked down and the door assembly was twisting. And in the keyhole, I saw something moving. He was using the knife to try and break the lock. The tip of the blade was visible as he twisted and pried.

My mind immediately went back to a conversation I had with my girlfriend months before. "He's broken many of the locks in the house so my mother cannot get away from him. The only two that still work are my bedroom door and the front door." Her voice echoed in my head. If he'd already broken all the other locks, this one probably wouldn't hold for long. I glanced around once more and got another idea. Running across the room, I picked up the mattress and wedged it in front of the door. Then we moved a few pieces of furniture in behind it. It wasn't much of a barricade, but it would slow him down. Plus, it was all we had.

The lock was clicking and popping.

Thinking quickly, I said, "We need to call the police. Do you have your phone?"

My girlfriend shook her head, "I do, but we can't call them."

"Why not?" I exclaim.

"If they come and see everything, they will see that he is beaten up. They will not take him; they will take you."

I realized she was right, and I wasn't at all interested in spending the night in a Polish jail. However, I was also not at all interested in being stabbed.

He kept working at the lock, but it held. Eventually, he went quiet. Not knowing what would happen next, I packed all my stuff. If we got out of there safely, I never wanted to step foot in that house again.

For two hours we waited, but nothing more happened. My girl-friend's mother decided to break the stalemate. We removed the barricade and peered through the keyhole, but he was nowhere to be seen. We unlocked the door and her mother slipped quietly out, pulling it shut behind her. We listened for any sign of disturbance but all we heard was a calm conversation from the other room. Maybe he had sobered up enough to be rational. My girlfriend listened for a minute then said, "She's tending his wounds." We waited a little longer to make sure he wouldn't get violent again. Then we grabbed our things and prepared to leave. Quietly we slipped into the hall-way, but before we made our break for it, I glanced into the living room. He was lying on the sofa, nursing his wounds with a damp towel. Standing next to him was his wife, mop in hand, dutifully cleaning his vomit, piss, and now blood off of the floor.

We took three steps down the hallway, made our way through the front door, and finally we were safe.

As we walked down the stairs, I couldn't help but ask, "How has she stayed with him for so long?"

"I've asked her that so many times," my girlfriend replied, "and her answer is always the same. 'He wasn't always like this.'"

"So, she's in love with the man he used to be, even though that man is now gone?" I asked.

She didn't answer.

We walked on for a while in silence, not sure where we were going. So we decided to get lunch, then go to an afternoon movie. We just wanted to unwind and not think about all this for a few hours.

I wish that was the end of the story.

After the movie we turned our phones back on. Hers immedi-ately started blowing up with text messages from her mom. Appar-ently after we'd left, he'd started drinking again. So she was pleading with us to come back and help her. Despite everything in me that screamed don't go back, we went back.

As we walked into the house, I saw that both he and her mother were in the kitchen. As soon as he saw me, he tore open a nearby drawer and took out a butcher knife. Quickly reversing it to hold the blade in his fingers, he pulled his arm back, threatening to throw it. Once again, I was faced with a terrible internal decision. But after weighing the odds, I decided it was best to ignore him and just make my way back into the bedroom. I closed and locked the door behind me but listened closely in case I needed to intercede. Things went reasonably well for the next 30 minutes or so, but then tensions flared once again. I opened the bedroom door and saw that he had returned to the living room. Once again, he faced off with my girlfriend. I looked down at his hands and am relieved to see he doesn't have a knife this time. Things seemed more stable than before, but then my girlfriend sprang to the right and dashed towards his desk.

I realized she was trying to get to one of the knives she told me he kept hidden around the house. As she sprinted past, he reached out and caught her by the ponytail, pulling with all his strength. She was yanked backward and spun around. Still holding her ponytail in his right hand, he hauled back with his left hand and punched her in the face as hard as he could. She screamed a blood curdling scream and time slowed down again.

I flew across the hallway into the living room.

His second punch smashed straight in her face.

I took two steps towards them.

His third punch was loaded and ready to fire.

I jumped on his back, right arm wrapping around his neck, left arm shooting under his left armpit then flipping upwards to lock in behind his head. I felt his punch launch and fizzle.

I got him wrapped up, but for the first time, I felt how strong he was. He may have been older and soft from alcohol, but at his core he was a bear. Just then my feet found the floor. Instinctively my right foot stepped back, and I bent my knees to pull him off balance. Then turning and exploding upwards, I used my left hip to leverage him into a jujitsu throw. But I didn't realize there wasn't enough space, so my right buttock smashed into his desk midway through the throw. It destabilized us both and we fell heavily to the floor. I held his neck tightly through it all and the moment we landed, I popped to one knee. Swinging my left leg over the top of him, I pinned him belly down on the floor. I established a rear naked choke. My right hand grabbed the inside of my left elbow, while my left grabbed the back of his head and pressed forward. From there he was virtually defenseless, but he was still trying to punch me. I inhaled deeply to inflate my chest, then applied the choke, cinching both my arms tightly around his throat. His face turned a bright cherry red, and his whole body tightened. Then I felt unconsciousness begin to take him. His body slowly relaxed, his raised fist lowering to the ground. As I felt him going out, I loosened the choke, allowing the blood to return to his brain.

But the second he woke, he immediately started punching at me again, so I cinched the choke once more. This time, I let him pass out completely before releasing. He "fell asleep" for a few seconds before snapping back. Finally, he seemed to realize it was over. He stopped fighting. This gave me a chance to take in the scene. The first thing I noticed was we were covered in blood. During the struggle his facial wounds from earlier had opened up. I watched as blood dripped steadily off the tip of his nose. I still had him in a light choke hold, keeping him in submission. I looked up at my girlfriend and her mother who were now standing beside us and calmly asked her to translate for me. My girlfriend nodded silently, her expression telling me to proceed.

"The way you've behaved today is not acceptable."

gf: "Twój dzisiejszy sposób zachowania jest niedopuszczalny."

"This is not how a man treats his family."

gf: "Nie tak człowiek traktuje swoją rodzinę"

"You need to make a deep change within yourself, because if you don't, someday you'll be an old man and all alone."

gf: "Musisz dokonać głębokiej zmiany w sobie, ponieważ jeśli nie któregoś dnia, będziesz starcem i zupełnie sam."

He didn't say anything in answer, but he was relaxed and docile. I let go of the choke hold and sat up, but I stayed on top of him in case he turned. His wife stooped down to doctor his face once again. She was a saint. When it felt safe to do so, I stood up and walked to the kitchen. Turning on the water, I grabbed a white bar of soap and began to wash his blood off my arms. Pinkish froth formed as I scrubbed.

Everything after that was foggy, but I do know we stayed in the house for the rest of the trip. He was on his best behavior for the remainder of our visit. I vowed I would never visit again, and I didn't.

My girlfriend and I broke up about a year after this. Too many of the things she'd suffered as a child stayed with her, like shadows of her father hovering over our every disagreement. I had believed naively that with enough love and understanding, she'd be able to recover. But that was not to be. If anything, I began to feel pulled ever more towards that kind of toxicity in my own actions, and that's when I had to go.

I later heard that her parents separated. Her father had returned to his normal routine of abuse after we'd left. I was glad to hear her mom got out. I hope she went on to find some happiness.

Bill Berry

Chapter 42

Auschwitz

No matter how many times you've seen it in the movies and no matter how many history books you've read, nothing can prepare you for the moment when you see it with your own eyes. My god... To my right was a forest of brick chimneys, easily hundreds of them, maybe even thousands of them, but not one of them attached to a serviceable structure. These brick sentinels, still blackened by the fires that once raged there stood vigil over the wreckage of the structures they once served. The wreckage that has lain undisturbed for so many decades it has begun to melt into the earth. My eyes tracked outwards, peering towards the farthest reaches of the compound, but the chimneys had no end. Their ethereal forms only disappeared because of a light fog near the horizon.

I looked left and saw six strange concrete structures, each standing two feet tall, four feet wide, but as long as a football field. On top of each structure were hundreds of holes, each the size of a medium pizza, openings that once served as communal toilets for some of the 130,000 residents who were imprisoned there. And like the view to the right, the wreckage also reached as far as the eye could see.

Straight ahead, I saw the lines of the dilapidated railroad tracks as they snaked across the landscape. This was the end of the line for so many. And as bad as the other parts of the camp must have been, I know that what lies at the end of these tracks was the most inconceivable thing of all. I began the walk, a journey that tens of thousands before me have made, but unlike them, death was not waiting for me at its end. The quiet was unsettling, even the birds knew not to sing here. The foggy air smelled of despair; anguish was permanently infused in the soil. Ahead I saw the rubble of several large buildings that were hastily destroyed in the hopes of hiding what had happened here, buildings that had once served as gas chambers and crematoriums. This place was built with one purpose, to eradicate entire populations. And that's what the nearly defeated Nazis wanted to hide, a place they'd hoped would be overlooked by the liberators. But there was no hiding a city sized factory of death. And this place forever stands as a reminder of what happened. Six million silenced voices must forever be a warning to future generations. May their sacrifice help us to understand that when peace is not possible, when tyrants become unreasonable, and when genocide appears on our earth, it must be stopped.

Chapter 43

Dollar Debacle

The large glass doors slid open, and the familiar smell of damp lumber greeted my nostrils. Ahead I saw two employees chatting, their bright orange vests branded them as DIY experts. I turned towards the long row of bright blue shopping carts and selected one that rolled smoothly. Reaching into my pocket I grabbed my list, but just then a greenish rectangle on the floor caught my eye.

Leaning down I saw George Washington's tight-lipped smirk. Suspicions confirmed I picked up the folded $1 bill. Glancing around, I saw no one who might be the potential owner, and the store was all but empty. So, I walked towards the two men, dollar in hand, blue cart trailing behind me.

As I got closer, I overheard one of them say "I better get back to it." Then he wandered off. The remaining guy was rummaging through a box of hinges. His vest read "Hi, I'm *DAVID*," but the David part was written in black Sharpie.

In a neutral tone I asked, "Hey David, is there a lost and found?"

David looked at me, then nodded his head towards the far side of the store and said, "Yeah, talk to the customer service desk. It's by the garden center. What did you lose?"

"I wanted to turn something in," I said.

"Oh, well I'm headed that way after I finish this. If you want, I can drop it off," he offered.

"Sure," I replied, handing him the dollar bill.

David looked at it and laughed, then he tried to hand it back.

Holding my hands up in the air I said, "It's not mine." Then I walked away.

I wandered the store for the next 25-30 minutes, loading the cart with things from my list. Then, I made my way to the checkout. Only one register was open, and the cashier was helping someone with a lot of items, so I waited. But after a few moments I noticed David walking slowly towards me. He seemed uneasy.

Without preamble, he said, "You've left me with quite the moral dilemma."

"How so?" I asked.

"Well," he said, "You've given me this dollar that you found. But here's the problem. If I go to lost and found with this and say I want to turn it in, they're going to laugh at me. And if I insist that they take it, they'll just put it in their pocket and keep it. But if I keep it myself, I'm going to feel terrible because you've done the right thing. So, I think it would be better for everyone if you just keep the dollar."

He held the dollar out to me expectantly.

Genuinely sympathetic I said, "But it's not mine."

With incredulity, David said, "Please, I don't want it. Would you please just take it?"

I shook my head gently from side to side and said, "It's not mine."

With a defeated look, David sighed. We stood there in silence for a few moments. Then David's expression brightened, "How about this? What if I take it to church on Sunday and drop it on the offering plate? That way it's out of our hands. We can leave it to God to decide what happens to it. How does that sound?"

With a shrug and a smile, I said, "It's not mine."

The person ahead of me finished and the cashier called, "Next."

David tilted his head back and stared at the ceiling as if seeking divine guidance. Then he looked at me one last time and said, "Okay, that's what I'll do. But I don't understand. Why won't you just take it?"

I studied his face for a moment before answering, "It's not mine."

My actions may have seemed strange to David that day, but my convictions align with my experiences. When I was very young, my mother took me to the grocery store. As we were checking out, I picked up a package of gum and asked her to buy it for me. She told me to put it back, but because I wanted it, I sneakily put it in my pocket instead. I was young, but I knew that stealing was wrong. It just seemed like such a small thing though, so I decided to chance it. Once we'd made it to the car, my childhood impatience got the better of me and before we'd even pulled out of our parking spot, I pulled out the gum. My mom put two and two together and told me I was going to have to return it. In front of a whole line of shoppers waiting to check out, I was made to articulate what I'd done and apologize for my actions. The clerk shook her head disapprovingly and then told me to put it back, which I did. It was terribly embarrassing, and I feel keyed up thinking about it even now decades later. It was a lesson I'll never forget.

Things have changed so much in the world since then. If a child of mine did the same thing today, I'd want to march them back in to teach them the same lesson I was taught. But nowadays I'd also be worried the clerk might not see it for the wonderful life lesson it is. What if they called the police and my child ended up with community service or on probation or who knows what? Some might even say the clerk would be justified in doing so because stealing is wrong. And yes, stealing is wrong, but when did we lose sight of something more important than the absolute letter of the law? Building an honest collaborative society.

Chapter 44

Behind a Bus

I put on my blinker and merged into the left turn lane, then slowed to a stop behind a big school bus. As I waited for the light to turn green, my eye was drawn to movement in the back of the bus. Like something out of a cartoon, I saw a boy's head creep slowly up from behind the bus's rear-most seat. With a gleam in his eye, he surveyed the scene, then with exaggerated slowness, he lowered his head back behind the seat. I felt the tension build. I knew something was coming, but what? Suddenly I saw both of his hands shoot out into the aisle between the seats. Waving wildly, he threw me a double fisted one finger victory salute. His message was clear, "Fuck you!" Then his hands darted back behind the safety of the seat. A few moments passed before he poked his head back into view, checking to see my reaction. I knew he couldn't see my eyes behind the dark sunglasses, and with my blank expression, there was zero indication that I had seen his display. A slight sigh slumped his shoulders.

I let his disappointment settle in for a few seconds, then I reached my right hand upwards, index finger extended. Curious now, his eyes followed my finger as I inserted it into my right nostril. Realizing what he was seeing, his eyes widened. Pushing harder, I dug as deeply into my nose as humanly possible. His jaw dropped open. He couldn't believe what he was seeing. Twisting now, I dug as hard as I could, then lifted my finger before my eyes for examination. Slowly, I popped my now wet finger right in my mouth. Every emotion known to man exploded across his face, disgust, glee, and more. In response, he screamed, turned, and fell backward into his seat. His outburst alerted the other students on the bus, and he excitedly tried to articulate what he had just witnessed. Suddenly half a dozen young faces are pressed up against the glass, hoping to catch a glimpse. But all they saw was a blank faced guy in dark sunglasses, holding his steering wheel with both hands, not doing anything out of the ordinary. The faces slowly fell as they realized the trickster on the bus had gotten them once again. I saw them shaking their heads in disappointment as they walked back to their seats. The boy raised his hands and continued pointing, clearly trying to convince them that it had really happened and that he hadn't made it up. But he wasn't fooling anyone. I knew what they were thinking, "What sane adult would ever pick their nose and eat it? Give it up prankster kid. We're not falling for it." Having lost his audience, and all credibility, the boy looked back out the window at me, an injured expression on his face. Then he raised both hands as if to say, "Come on man, why didn't you show them?" Again, I sat expressionless, giving no indication that I even saw him. Then the light turned green, the bus began its turn, and the boy rolled out of my life forever.

In life, there will be road rage, flipped fingers, and hateful words thrown your way. When that happens, you can rise to the occasion, amplify the anger, throw it back at them, and defend your honor. Or maybe you can turn it all on its head. When he flipped me off, I could have gotten angry or just ignored him. But instead, I chose to play and make fun of the situation, which seems like a much better way to live. So, keep this handy the next time someone wants to fight you, curses at you, or whatever; just reach up and pick your nose. It can be a great social lubricant.

Oh, one last thing, if you're reading this Mr. back of the bus prankster kid; this is my confession. Yes, it was me, and I did eat it.

Chapter 45

7, 6, 5, ::ding::

7, 6, 5, ding, the elevator doors opened, and I saw an elderly woman standing behind a man in a wheelchair. They looked to be in their 70s, so I held the door for them while they boarded. She thanked me and asked if I'd press, "Two please." I did, and the doors inched closed. The man sat quietly with his arms pulled tightly against his chest, his head slumped unnaturally to one side. He did not move. 5, 4, 3, as we descended, she reached down and carefully pushed back a lock of his hair that had fallen out of place. It was a small thing, but with that gesture, she conveyed a love that nearly brought me to tears. 3, 2, ding. The doors opened and carefully she backed him out of the elevator, smiling pleasantly as she went. I watched them move down the hallway, then the doors closed, and they were gone.

We cannot know if one day we'll be the one in the chair, or the one pushing it. But I know this, true love is not caring which part you'll play, only that you'll play those parts together.

Chapter 46

Instant Karma

My friend and I had just finished our meal and one of the many crew members began to collect our plates. Glancing up at her name tag, I saw that she was from Moldova. I had been working on cruise ships for years at that point, but it was the first time I had seen anyone from Moldova.

"Thank you," I said.

"Yur're Velcome," she responded in a thick Slavic accent.

"I just noticed your name tag," I continued. "Where is Moldova?"

She stacked the last of our dishes on an already full bus tray, and without making eye contact said, "Ov course yu don't know vare Moldova iz. Yu are Amedican and Amedicans don't learn about anyting but Amedica."

I was surprised by her directness, but I didn't disagree with what she had said. Our education in my experience was largely centered on national interests.

Without pause she continued her beration, "Yu are unedukated, yu don't know about ze vurld outzide of Amedica. But yu think yu own ze whole vurld and can do anyzing yu vant."

She walked backward as she spoke, continuing her attack even as

158

she moved to her next task. "Yu are stupidz, STUPIDZ Amedicans." Then turning triumphantly on her heels, she walked straight into a big steel support pole. The dishes on the tray clinked alarmingly but somehow stayed in place. Standing face-to-face with the pole, her proud chin lowered, and her shoulders slumped in embarrassment. We could hear her unspoken thoughts, "Oh my god, I was just telling them how stupid they are, and then I walk into a pole. Ugh!" She stood there a moment longer than necessary, a silent acknowledgment of the instant karma the universe had just dealt. Then, with a ballet dancer's grace, she stood tall as ever and took an exaggerated step to the side. She continued around the pole and back to the dirty dish station. My friend and I looked at each other for the briefest of moments but had to look away to stop from laughing. It was a deep insistent laughter, but we both fought to hold it back. When she walked into the pole, it undid all the meanness she had initially sent our way. So, if we'd have laughed in her presence, it would have unleveled the field again. Still, it was exploding out of us. My chest started shaking in the effort to hold it back. Without making eye contact, I casually pointed toward the exit, the universal symbol of, "Let's get out of here." We both managed to hold our composure until we exited the buffet and made it to the outside pool deck. No one was around and we finally were able to let the laughter explode out of us. After we'd let it all out, we continued about our business.

Two days later we were sitting in the buffet again and the same waitress was assigned to our table. She walked over to us and asked if we needed anything. Her demeanor was completely different this time, and she was very nice throughout. Even telling us some interesting things about her home country of Moldova. She helped us learn a little more about her world. I admired her effort. Sometimes when we do something embarrassing or speak in a way that we later regret, it's easy to want to avoid any further interactions. But she didn't shy away, and I respect that, so we never said a word about the incident.

Growing up my mom had a saying, "Everyone is entitled to a bad

day now and then, so don't take it personally."
    There's a lot of wisdom in that.

Chapter 47

Rape in Jamaica

As we walked down the streets of Jamaica, we passed dozens of cab drivers. Most of them pitched their services aggressively, all but shoving you into their cabs while promising to take you to the best beach or bar on the island. But I was a seasoned traveler; I knew we were just a fare to them. One more group of tourists among the thousands who visit each year. We were three more faces they wouldn't recognize a few hours later. And that wasn't what I was looking for. Maybe I wasn't sure what we were looking for, but it wasn't that. So, I kept on until we had passed the majority of drivers. But then I heard a soft voice from behind me, "Why ____ ____ rubber when _____ ____ ____ mine?"

Not understanding what the man had said, I turned and asked, "What was that?"

"I said, why burn your rubber when you can burn mine," he repeated.

Half confused by his comment, and half recovering from the sight of the man before me, I stupidly asked, "Uhhh, what?"

Pointing to my flip flops now he repeated, "Why burn your

rubber," then pointing to the wheels of his cab, "when you can burn mine?"

I instantly smiled, in part because his pitch was clever, in part because this soft voice was emanating from one of the largest human beings I had ever seen. "Is there a beach where none of the tourists go," I asked. "Like, if you and your family went to the beach, where would you go?"

The cabbie thought for a moment, then said, "Ahhh, Rainbow Beach. It's not far. You could walk it in 15 minutes."

Looking at my two friends I asked, "What do you think?" They both nodded in agreement, so I turned to the driver and said, "Can we ride with you?"

The man had been leaning on the fender of his white minivan but now stood to his full 6'5" height. Reaching out an arm that was black as night and big as my thigh, he opened the passenger door and said, "When the student is ready, the teacher will appear."

I liked him already.

After we climbed in, he closed our doors and casually made his way around to the driver's side. He was an easy 300 pounds but carried himself with ease. Once seated he pulled the driver's side seatbelt as far forward as it would reach, then wrapped it around his bulk. Checking each of his mirrors for traffic he said, "Alright, Rainbow Beach."

Along the way the driver and I chatted about Jamaican politics, philosophy, and life. I learned that before starting the cab company with his brothers he'd been a police officer, then later he became a special operative tasked with guarding important political figures and visiting dignitaries. I asked him what his daily carry weapon had been and with a surprised look he asked, "You know guns?

"A little," I said, "Back home I'm a member of a shooting club and I enjoy target shooting."

Looking even more surprised, but also pleased, he asked, "Do you know Desert Eagle?"

Laughing out loud I said, "Desert Eagle .50, of course!"

It was his turn to laugh, and it was one of those laughs that only enlightened or genuinely grateful people emit. Then he lifted his white button-down shirt to reveal a semiautomatic handgun tucked into his waistband. I can clearly see it's a Desert Eagle .50.

If you're a gun enthusiast, then you already know this, but if you aren't here are the facts. When a movie maker wants to show that one of their characters is a total badass, they will often portray that character with a .50 caliber Desert Eagle. The handgun itself is comically big, with a load so powerful, few mortals can actually wield it. But even if someone could put rounds on target, few could afford to. It would cost 20 bucks just to cycle through a 7+1 mag. It's the pinnacle of shock and awe, but no one really carries one in real life, or at least that's what I'd believed up until that moment.

Looking him in the eyes I said, "So you're a taxi driver, philosopher, and bodyguard."

He smiled broadly revealing teeth that were clearly an adult's but look more like baby teeth in his oversized jaw. "When you ride with me you become family, and I take care of my family."

We held eye contact for a few moments, then I reached my hand out and asked, "What's your name?"

Enveloping my hand in his he said, "Winston _____ (last name omitted for anonymity), and you?"

"Bill Berry," I answer.

"Bill Berry," he repeated out loud. And with those words I knew I had made a lifelong friend.

We turned onto a dirt road that led to the beach. I saw a small sign nailed to a palm tree. Its once bright red, green, and yellow Rastafarian colors were faded, but it clearly read Rainbow Beach in roughly painted letters.

We stopped in a small dirt parking lot. There were no designated spots, but that wasn't a problem since we were the only car there. The view out my passenger's window looked like a postcard come to life. There was a long, picturesque shore with gleaming white sand. Palm trees and shrubs hugged the high tide mark, and perfectly completing the scene was a young black couple walking hand in hand about 100 yards down the beach. They looked like newlyweds exploring Paradise Island.

Gathering our gear, we stepped out of the cab. Winston met us as we debarked and pointed up the beach, "If you need anything, these guys will look after you."

I was about to ask, "What guys," when I saw two dark skinned wiry looking men step out from the tree line. They gave a friendly wave then pointed to a concession stand they had built a little way up the beach. Really it was just an old wooden table next to a faded ice chest bristling with bottled water and an assortment of beers.

With an inviting sweep of his arm Winston said, "Enjoy yourselves! I will be back in two hours."

I nodded and thanked him, confident that he would actually be back at the designated time. Then we made our way down to the water to don our masks and fins for a snorkeling adventure.

The waters off Rainbow Beach didn't disappoint. We saw countless colorful fish and corals as we lazily drifted along the coastline. But sooner than we would have liked, it was time to go. So, the three of us swam to the shore only to realize we'd traveled a good mile away from where we'd started. Not wanting the moment to end yet, my one friend said, "I'm going to swim back." Then he reseated his mask and dove into the water. I was tempted to join him but saw that our other friend was tired, so I decided to walk back and keep him company. We'd made it about a quarter mile when I heard a loud crashing sound from the tree line to our left. Bracing myself in case a wild animal was preparing to attack us, I peered into the brush. I picked up some movement and quickly realized that it was the young couple we'd seen walking on the beach when we'd first arrived. But now they were scuffling on the ground. At first, I thought they were having sex, but everything about it felt wrong. It was too aggressive, too frantic.

The woman turned her head and seeing us screamed, "Help! Help me!" Startled, the man looked over at us, too. She used the moment to intensify her struggle. Bucking her hips, he lost balance allowing her to roll out from under him. Leaping to her feet her screams turned to whimpering sobs, "Please, help me!" Before she could get away, he caught her by the wrist, but seeing us there had given her new strength. She tore herself free. Sprinting out of the trees I saw the wet lines of tears streaked across her dark cheeks. Her arms reached out with the clear intention of bear hugging me in thanks and desperation. But right before she got to me, I stepped to the left and swung my right arm across my body to sweep her hands to the side. Then placing my right hand on her right shoulder, I pushed gently allowing the momentum to carry her into the arms of my friend behind me. I wanted to comfort her of course, but I couldn't do that and deal with her attacker at the same time. The man who'd been holding her ran out of the trees. He was intent on reclaiming his prize. But as soon as we made eye contact, he changed his tact. "No, no! It's a misunderstanding, just let me talk to you!"

Hearing this, the woman started screaming, "Misunderstanding! Misunderstanding! You were trying to rape me! Fuck You! *Fuck-kkkkkk Youuuuuuu!*"

The man continued to explain himself, even sidestepping as if he intended to go around me, but I stepped in front of him, making it clear that he was no longer in control. But then, emboldened by our presence, the woman charged back around me and started hitting the man, all the while screaming, "Fuck You! Get away from me! *Fuuucckk Yooouuuu!*"

She continued her assault, and I saw he was getting angry but didn't dare hit her now that we were there. She shoved him a few more times then moved between us to tell us what happened.

"I met him outside my hotel. He said he'd show me around, and I said yes because my friend who was supposed to be here had to cancel. But I still wanted to come, so we went to lunch, then we came here. I should have known. I should have known when I had to pay for everything because he had no money. I'm from Ethiopia; I knew! Why was I so stupid? I don't know what I would have done if you guys hadn't come. He would have raped me. He *was* raping me. Oh my God!" Then turning to look back at the man still following behind she screamed, "Dude, fuck you! Get the fuck away from me!"

All through this my friend and I stood on each side of her, steadily making our way back to the parking lot where we'd been dropped off a few hours ago. I was hoping that the two men working concessions would help us. But then again, maybe they knew this guy and were in on it. Fuck, then it would be three of them against four of us with her included. Which was still manageable unless they had weapons. I realized there were still a lot of ways it could go badly.

Luckily within minutes of arriving back at the small dirt parking lot, Winston came to collect us. He opened the doors for us, and we motioned for the woman to board first. Then we climbed in behind her. Audaciously the man tried to get in with us, but Winston closed the doors before he had a chance. The man started to argue, waving his hands, but then Winston whispered ominously, "Fuck off, man." The man backed away. Winston stood there immobile until the man had retreated a respectable distance, and then he made his way back around to the driver's side door. Climbing in he once again pulled the seatbelt strap far out in front of himself, checked his mirrors, and headed back towards the road. It was quiet in the van, the post adrenaline calm that often follows hair raising experiences. Winston broke the silence, "So, did we have fun at the beach?"

* * *

I feel as though I've been prepared for moments like these since childhood. When I was young, I started having terrible recurring nightmares. I'd find myself lying on the floor of a church, the cold of the tiles piercing my bones. I'd see a gunman's feet several pews away. The sharp squeaks of his monochrome black Converse echo through the cathedral each time he turns. There are people all around, all having hit the deck when he pulled the gun. An old woman in the row next to mine is wearing a knitted green long sleeve sweater, but I can't see her face. The gunman screams, and his first shots ring out. People scream in terror, some try to run, while others huddle frozen in place. I hear bodies falling, but from the shots or taking cover, I don't know which. Time slows, which feels familiar, though I can't place why. More shots sound, but I feel no fear. It's not that it left, it just wasn't there at all. A sense of purpose fills me. I'm on my feet, running towards the front of the room. Not for the exit or safety, but straight at the man. This is where the dream changes. Sometimes I wrestle the gun from him and live. Sometimes I am immediately shot but still manage to stop him, helped by others who jump in to take him down. And sometimes, I'd see his arm raise in my direction, multiple shots soundlessly fire as he squeezes off round after round. I feel the impact in my chest. Falling to the floor I see the lady in the green sweater. She's motionless now, a thin stream of blood seeping from beneath her fingers, slowly oozing its way downhill toward me and the pulpit. The cold of the floor chills me again. My joints feel frozen. I try to stand but can't. A circle of darkness narrows my vision. I realize I've failed, and I feel sad. Then I die.

I would usually startle awake in my bed, realizing it was another nightmare.

It happened once every month or two, possibly for a few years. Each time it happened, I would try to crack the code to come out on top. But no matter what I did, the result was unpredictable. There was no solution that guaranteed my safety. But sometimes, when I'd win, the little old lady in the green sweater would live. I'd never get to see her face, but I'd see her standing again, alive and well.

One day after waking from this nightmare, I decided to say a little prayer.

"God, if this is your message, if you're asking me to accept that one day, I might be called upon to do something requiring my own sacrifice, I accept. Whatever it is, when it comes, I will not turn away."

Once I accepted that call, I never had the dream again. In that moment I decided to say yes to whatever life presented me with, even if that thing could end my life.

When the girl on the beach ran up to me with the rapist hot on her heels, I heard that voice in my head. "I will not turn away."

Some of the things you'll read in these pages is a reflection of that moment and that vow. I believe I've been put here for a reason, and I will not miss it when it comes.

Chapter 48

Extending a Hand

The wooden ladder was homemade. It was a patchwork of 2x4s and deck screws that were probably serviceable when some Jamaican tour operator first placed it there. But the hundreds of visitors and salty sea air had taken their toll. Its top rungs were broken and dangling at unnatural angles. Rusty screws protruded ominously, looking like little booby traps ready to grab any clothing or flesh that came near. Originally it reached all the way to the top of the cliff face, allowing visitors to enjoy the view from the top of the waterfall. But now if you wanted to reach the top, you had to climb the last section of the cliff on your own. Reaching my left hand out, I grabbed a piece of tree root that had been exposed by wind and erosion. Then leaning off the side of the ladder, I pressed/levered myself up high enough to transition from the ladder to land. It was doable but sketchy. It was unsettling to think they were bringing tourists there. A slip would give you a quick view of the falls before you fell two stories to the rocks below. Scooting myself over the top I reached a flat area that felt safe. I just had to make sure everyone else made it up okay.

Turning and looking back down, I saw a man with thinning grey hair start his climb. He was about 65, strong, and wiry looking. But as he approached the top, he discovered the same problems I did, except, his arms were too short to reach the tree root I'd used to dismount. He felt along the rocky edge trying to find something solid. I knew there wasn't much there for him to use, so I braced myself firmly, leaned over, and extended my hand. He looked at it, evaluating its possibility, but quickly waved me off. I couldn't blame him. It was a scary situation. I started to pull my hand back, but something inside me stopped it. Instead, I stood fast, helpful hand still extended, but also wondered in the back of my mind if I was being insulting by ignoring his dismissal. Continuing the search he found a small handhold, then lifted himself off the ladder. He was looking good, but then the awkwardness of the angle shifted his weight. His body started to pivot, and gravity was twisting him off the rock face. I watched his eyes grow wide. The realization of what is happening hits him: he is falling. Instinctually, his hand shot out for the only thing that might stop him, my hand. The sudden weight was jarring. I felt myself drug forward, but my initial position was stable enough to arrest the fall. We teetered for a moment, pondering our new positions. Then, pulling hard against me, he managed to turn himself back flat against the rock face. His feet found something to push against and in a panic, he willed himself upwards over the jagged rocks. I pulled in unison, inching him higher and higher until he finally found a balanced position. Neither of us said anything at first, but once the adrenaline started to fade he looked me in the eye and simply said, "Thank you."

"No worries," I answered. "Not sure the waterfall was worth that."

He smiles and nods but doesn't answer as he pulls himself the last little ways up to safety.

Once he settled in, I went back to the edge to help the next two people get to the top. As I waited for them, I thought about how close we'd just come to an accident. If I'd pulled my hand back when he waved me off, he very well could have fallen. The realization felt heavy in my stomach, and I decided right then to never withdraw my hand once offered. If you, "extend a helping hand" to someone in need, be that a literal or figurative hand, let it be your bond. Because even if they don't need it right then, they might a moment later. No matter what, don't pull it back, because the future is an unpredictable place.

One of the two women who'd been below neared the top, and realizing the ladder's dilemma. She asked, "How did you get up there?"

Leaning over I extended my hand, and this time I insisted she take it.

Chapter 49

A Casual Sexual Assault

I was practicing yoga in the passenger gym while working onboard a cruise ship. These practices often included advanced postures, so it was common for people to stop and watch. One day during this practice, I noticed an elderly man observing me but didn't think much of it. Eventually, I closed my practice and began to roll up my mat. That's when the grey-haired gentlemen ambled over and reached down to shake my hand.

Speaking in a thick old-world accent he said, "Very good. you are a pleasure to watch."

I was still half crouched on the ground collecting my things, but he continued pulling and shaking my hand saying, "You must have practiced for many years."

As he was shaking my hand, he began to push his crotch forward so that with each of his emphatic handshakes, the backs of my fingers began to graze his privates. I was shocked and assumed it was surely happening on accident, but then he pulled my hand in even farther, to the point that I could feel his hardening penis.

I firmly pulled my hand back, breaking his grip. His smile

vanished, and in a lowered tone he growled, "I'll be in the sauna," then he walked away.

I felt numb, disrespected, and violated.

I sat there for a minute, trying to figure out what to do. I was an employee on the ship at the time, so I considered talking to one of my higher-ups, but I immediately thought better of it.

What was I going to say? "An old man grabbed my hand and rubbed it against his penis!" It would be my word against his. The whole situation would be awkward, and management might view me as the one causing problems by coming forward. It wasn't hard to imagine the loss of future contracts over something like this. So, I made my decision, and I did what many of us might do in the same circumstances. I acted like it never happened.

Looking back, I'm still floored that someone could be so miscalibrated and brazen. I'm guessing he was around 60. How long has he been violating people like this? How many others have been put in this awkward situation?

Despite the violation, I felt a little sorry for him, too. What damages might he have suffered to have arrived at this place to think this behavior was acceptable? Then again, maybe he was slipping into the early phases of dementia. Or maybe I'm just making excuses for him, which is an easy thing to fall into. I'll never know for sure.

Chapter 50

Bosnia

W e'd landed in Bosnia and were on our way to a military base to perform. As we drove, we passed a block long apartment complex. It was three stories tall and bereft of decor. As we traveled beside it, I saw that the entire center of the building had been obliterated. Sometime before, a bomb had landed in the middle and blasted an upside-down mushroom shape in the structure. Rusty rebar and broken pipes protruded from the torn concrete edges. Numerous residences were missing. Despite this, people were still living in the surrounding units. One family was sitting lazily in a "bedroom" that had been transformed into a balcony when its walls collapsed. They'd pulled the rebar that stuck out of the floor upwards to form a crude railing. And a young boy having stuck his legs between the bars was sat on its edge, bare feet dangling freely. From where he sat, he could look over the open space where his neighbors' units used to be. Other families had run clotheslines across the open space. Their button-down shirts and jeans fluttered in the breeze, drying in what had once been someone's living room or kitchen. The utility of it all shook me. I guess I'd always imagined that after something like this happens there would be protocols. City officials would condemn the building, aid workers relocating residents to new lodging, and construction crews demolish everything in preparation for rebuilding. But now I saw that it wasn't like that at all. The reality left me feeling naive and idyllic. These people had nowhere else to go, so they continued on as best they could.

As the building faded behind us, war felt real to me for the first time. I started to imagine what it might have been like to come home from school when I was a kid, only to walk into my bedroom and find that half my room was gone. Would I also have sat on the floor in shock, dangling my feet over the crumbling edge? I probably would have.

Before that moment, war was Hollywood, history books, and courageous charges against the enemy. But as I watched that kid dangle his feet, I realized what it really was. Bombs don't care what they blow up. A bullet once fired can never be recalled. The lives of normal people, people just like me, can be destroyed in an instant. Utterly senseless. Moments like that make me want to meet god, because I have many questions.

Chapter 51

Too Small to Matter

I love long multi-day backpacking trips. Thirty miles or more, at least two to three nights out without re-supply. I want to be taken out of all my normal routines. I want my mind to discover new ways of thinking and have my body pushed into new ways of doing things. It was on one such trip, as my mind was transitioning from city mode to trail mode, that I was struck by a very small thought. "How can I make any difference in the world? I'm just a number, a blip on the cosmic timeline. What difference could my being here actually have?"

And though each step on the pine-needly forest floor carried me further into the wild, I remained trapped in my mind with these spiraling thoughts over meaning and purpose. Eventually, my internal musing was disturbed by the telltale sound of thousands of wing flaps per second. A mosquito was buzzing hungrily next to my ear and reflexively I swatted at it, but it evaded my efforts. I stopped walking, hoping to catch and squish the little beastie as it moved in for the attack. Predictably, once I stopped, it was nowhere to be seen. I quickly started off again, hoping to create some distance between us, but thirty seconds later, it had caught up.

Realizing nature's 2.5-milligram scourge wasn't likely to give up, I un-slung my pack and dug out some bug spray. As I applied the stinky fluid to my arms, I was reminded of the meaninglessness I'd been so ardently pondering prior to the interruption. The smallness of my ability to impact the world around me. Right on cue, the mosquito buzzed in my ear again. And though I could hear the tiny wings, I felt no rush of air. There was no pain or bite upon my skin. Based on nothing but the sound of those tiny wings, I, a person roughly 36,287,360 times bigger in size, had been sent scurrying.

Nature is always ready to teach if only we're ready to listen. Suddenly I was thankful for the mosquito. Thankful for the realization that even the smallest of things can have a big effect on the world around them.

I admit, there are still days when I feel small. Still days when I'm left wondering how much of an impact I can have. But now when that happens, I think of this story, and it helps me feel a little less small.

Chapter 52

In the Name of

One time I met a very nice woman, and as we talked, she shared a very personal story with me. She had been sitting alone in her car at a red light. The light had turned green, but she didn't notice. So, the car behind her honked. She jumped, startled, and saw that the light had turned green. She started to go when a strong male voice from the back seat said, "Don't go!" She hesitated, but the car behind her honked again. She started to go again but the voice once again said, "Don't go!" She sat there wondering what was happening when all of a sudden, an 18-wheeler came barreling through the intersection. Immediately she realized that if she'd pulled out when the guy had honked the first or second time, she probably would have been smashed into oblivion.

She thanked God for speaking to her and saving her life. It was a moving story.

Normally this is where the story would end. But then she asked if I would pray with her, and I obliged. We all held hands and she said, "Thank you for bringing us together and guiding us through difficult situations. And thank you for our new friends. May we all know peace and joy through your love, in the name of Allah."

I was raised a Christian, so when she said Allah I was startled. I'd been taught to believe that all other religions were false. But on that day, I realized that people of all walks and all faiths hear the voice of God.

By this point in life I'd become an atheist, because the more I'd studied, the less religion made any sense to me. And though I'd grown confident that there was no God, I'd also heard that *voice* she spoke of when I'd been in life threatening situations.

It made me wonder. If there is a "creator" out there, it wouldn't condone the very human divisions we've made in the name of religion. The true God would speak equally to all, whether they carried a Bible, Koran, or nothing at all. And if we did away with all the divisions of religion, if we focused on being good to one another just because it's the right thing to do, then we'd be moving closer to the central message of nearly every religion that's ever existed. And that's something all humans can aspire to.

Chapter 53

Dexter

A lifetime ago a girlfriend of mine wanted a kitten. I love cats. They're my favorite animals, but I was traveling a lot at the time and couldn't take on the responsibility of looking after one. So, I distanced myself from it all and said, "If you decide to get one, it is your responsibility." She agreed to the terms and the very next day brought home a kitten. We named him Dexter, and he was the sweetest thing. But from the moment he got settled in, he cried and cried. She gave him food, water, and snuggles, but nothing helped. He cried all night and on into the morning. The next day she had to go to work and coincidentally he began to calm down and sleep a bit. I thought, "Oh good, he's doing better." He slept a bit more. And then some more, until I thought, this isn't normal. I came to the conclusion that he wasn't sleeping. I actually thought he was dying.

We were sharing a vehicle at the time, so I called my girlfriend for help. While I waited for her, I wrapped Dexter gently in a towel and met her in the parking lot so we could get to the vet as fast as possible, but we weren't fast enough. He died in my arms on the way. The vet still did an examination and explained to us what had gone wrong.

Dexter died from toxic shock because he had not gone to the bathroom. He explained that kittens this small will not go without permission from their momma. When you adopt them this young you have to rub their privates with a moist Q-Tip periodically to stimulate them. Neither of us had known that, and upon learning it I realized that he'd been trying to tell us all evening. He was saying, "It hurts, I have to go, please, I have to go to the bathroom!" But in our ignorance, we'd failed to grant him this simple request. And he suffered terribly because we didn't know. Because I didn't take the time to understand.

I'm sharing this story in the hope you won't repeat the same mistake yourself. And to encourage you to continually learn about anything and everything you can. Never miss out on an opportunity to learn. If you do enough and live enough, you'll see that everything you pick up along the way is useful eventually.

Chapter 54

Brother and Sister

After the heartbreak of losing a small kitten we'd adopted named Dexter, my girlfriend and I decided to try again. Keeping our ears open, it wasn't long before we came across an ad for some kittens needing a home. We went to the address, planning to adopt just one. But when we saw two of them snuggled together, we felt bad at the thought of separating them. The lady showing them said, "The mostly black one is the little girl, and the grey and black tiger striped one is her brother."

My girlfriend and I gave each other a knowing look then said to the lady, "We'll take them both."

"Ok great!"

We brought them home and never were two kittens more loved or spoiled. They got treats and snuggles and anything else they wanted.

The little girl we named Oreo, though her round-the-house nicknames were, "Bitty" for Itty Bitty girl, and "Princess" because "Your Highness" didn't roll off the tongue so well. She was pampered and played with delicately as was befitting a lady of her standing.

Her brother on the other hand, was a fireball. We called him Snickerdoodle (we were on a cookie themed naming kick that week), but his common name was "Noodles," or "Noodle Head." No sooner would I walk in the door and he'd be right there ready to fight. He loved to wrassle and play hard. Then, after he'd tire out, I'd sit down in my office chair to work, and Princess Bitty would grace me with her presence. Daintily climbing up, she'd fall asleep between my neck and the chair back while I worked, so cute.

Though siblings, they were polar opposites and the typical brother/sister feuds were frequent. Noodles would attack poor Bitty, and she'd cry out to be saved from his relentless assaults. No real damage was done during these bouts, but Bitty would often pout after, looking deeply insulted by the violence made against her person.

Different as they were, we loved them both through and through.

A few months later, they were old enough to be spayed and neutered. We called the vet to make an appointment, and when the day arrived, we took them in.

Once in the examination room the vet opened the carrier and to my surprise Bitty walked right out to say hello. The vet greeted her and since she was there already, did the examination, reporting to us that everything appeared normal.

Then the vet reached in to pull out Noodles. He struggled to stay in the carrier, but having had a lot of practice extracting kitties from carriers, she popped him out in short order. The examination began normally, but then the vet got a concerned look on her face. Walking over to the stack of paperwork she checked some notes, then over her shoulder she said to us, "You're here for a spay and neuter, correct?"

My girlfriend and I nodded and said, "Yes, that's why we're here."

The vet shook her head and said, "Well I'm sorry but we're not going to be able to do that."

We sat there confused, not understanding the problem.

The vet turned back towards us and raised her eyebrows, it felt like she was waiting for us to get something, but what that something was we had no clue.

In a tone that one might use when talking to an idiot, the vet said, "We can't do a spay and neuter because they're both girls."

I felt the fabric of the universe warp, then dumbly said, "But, the lady we adopted them from said they were brother and sister."

Trying to keep her cool, but lifting her eyebrows incredulously, the vet said, "You know it's plain as day, all you gotta do is look under the tail part."

I wanted to argue but realized that anything I could say in my defense would just make me look stupider. Eventually I shrugged my shoulders and said, "I guess we didn't think to look."

Picking up the stack of papers the vet asked, "So, I assume you'd like for me to adjust this paperwork to say SPAY for both of them?"

"That would seem most appropriate in light of these findings," I shot back.

Shaking her head side to side she said, "I'll write it up." Then she walked out of the examination room.

A technician came in and took the kitties to the back room. Then we were told we could pick them both up first thing in the morning.

On the drive home my girlfriend and I talked about what had happened.

"Looks like we have two little girls," She said.

"Yeah, two beautiful little girls."

"It's totally fine, but, doesn't it feel a little strange?" she asked.

It didn't matter to me that we actually had two girl cats now, I loved them both just the same. But she was right, there was something about it that felt odd. And I knew logically that the gender I'd assigned my cat was a designation I'd made in my own head, since I'd obviously not chosen Noodles gender based on the parts under his (her) tail. But it took time for my brain to adjust. I started thinking back to all the times I'd played so rough with him (her), how he'd (she'd) loved to wrassle, and how behaviorally I'd been so convinced he (she) was a boy. I even wondered how much I'd projected my own gender biases onto my cats, and how that might have impacted their personalities.

This was long before gender identity was an everyday news item. There were no resources available to cat dads dealing with this sort of news. But facts were facts, Noodles was no longer a boy; Noodles was now a girl.

My girlfriend continued thinking out loud, "Do we have to change his, I mean her name?"

"Is Noodles a gender neutral name?" I asked. "Either way, I don't think we need to change *her* name." I was happy to have thought of him as her for the first time.

It took a few days, but things felt normal again soon enough. For a few weeks I had this nagging feeling that I'd somehow lost a son. But I'd also gained a daughter. A rough and tumble, feisty as ever, tomboy of a daughter. But daughter nonetheless. And once they'd healed from their surgeries, life around the house was no different than it had been before. Noodles always wanted to wrassle, and Bitty continued to play the princess, meowing for help whenever her sister played too rough.

When my cat's gender changed, how I felt about them didn't change at all.

If anything, it helped me become aware of how much my own behavior had been influenced by the gender presumptions I'd made. And I was aware of how I treated them differently based on what I thought was or wasn't under their tails, despite them both being girls at heart.

Chapter 55

The Cost of Perfection

My buddy built a Sprinter van into a mobile camper/tiny home, and I'd stopped by to see it. While giving me a tour, this conversation unfolded:

Me: "What crack?"

Larry: "The one between the laminate and the baseboard."

Me: Peering closer, "Dude, that's invisible. I never would've seen it."

Larry: "Yeah, maybe, but I know it's there. I didn't account for the shrinkage of the vinyl when it gets hot, so I'm going to fix it."

Me: "How? You'd have to uninstall all this cabinetry."

Larry stares at me, his face reserved.

Me: "Omg, you're actually going to pull everything out and re-lay the floor?"

Larry: "Yeah, I know, but I have to make it perfect."

Me: "It's your build, but I'm telling you, it's not worth it."

A few months later we crossed paths again, and sure enough, he'd fixed the crack.

Me: "Hey, it looks good."

Larry: "Yeah, the crack is gone, but nothing else is right. When I put the countertop back in it didn't line up. So now I've got this gap behind the sink." As he said this, he pointed to a more glaring error than the one he'd originally been trying to fix.

"Plus, I had to peel the floor up and the adhesive isn't holding anymore, so there are these bubbles." He stepped on a spot the size of a small plate to show me how the floor would cave in and then pop back up again when there was no weight on it.

Neither of us had to say it, but his pursuit of perfection had caused problems far worse than the ones he'd initially started with.

No matter how hard we try, perfection can never be achieved.

But there's hope. People have been making their way in the world for eons without doing anything perfectly.

And you can too. Just remember these few tips.

1. Trust yourself: Perfect is unachievable, so do the best you can, in the time you have, with the resources you have available. Whatever comes out of it will be just right, and no one can ask for more, not even you.

2. Know when to stop: If you can do something in four hours and have it turn out 90% perfect, maybe that's enough. But if it's not enough, put four more hours into it so it's 95% perfect. And if that's still not enough, put four more hours into it so it's 97% perfect, then stop. The law of diminishing returns will weigh more and more heavily on you the farther you go. Don't fall into the trap.

3. Perfect is the enemy of great: While perfectionists often labor over one thing indefinitely, less obsessive creatives are cranking out huge bodies of "great" work. They're getting their "great" ideas out into the world. And they don't worry about it being perfect. They know that finished is better than perfect.

Don't let the pursuit of perfection hold you back from doing great work.

Chapter 56

What Motivates a Butterfly

While hiking in the Great Smokey Mountains, I came upon a patch of butterflies. Iridescent blue wings glittering in the sunlight, they'd gathered around a small pool to drink. A few feet down the trail from this kaleidoscope of color, I noticed another one by himself. Laying upside down, I thought he was dead, but then he moved a little. Scooting closer I saw yellowish guts hanging from his abdomen, probably the result of being stepped on by one of the many hikers passing by. Something about a butterfly dying on its back bothered me, so I picked him up and turned him right side up again, holding him delicately in my hand. With my finger, I caressed his tiny shoulders, hoping to impart some small measure of comfort. I knew the end was near, and my first thought was to end it quickly. But something about the serenity of the scene gave me pause. I wished I could have asked him what he wanted. If only I could speak butterfly. But even as I thought the words I realized my inability to speak butterfly was my own failing. I'd never taken the time to understand what motivates a butterfly, nor imagined a scenario where I'd need such information before this moment.

So, I asked him, without much hope of an answer, "What do you want my little friend? Talk to me." He sat in my hand looking forlorn, antennae twitching with a liveliness inconsistent with his broken body, but he said not a word. Hoping for some instruction, I set him near the other butterflies to see what he would do, to see if he would "tell me" what he wanted.

As soon as he was on the ground again, he began to crawl towards the other butterflies. They were gathered in a circle, drinking from the bits of mud. Soon enough he joined them at the "ol' watering hole." I watched for a minute or two as he sat with his friends enjoying a cool drink, then realized that this was his answer. So, I left him be.

As I walked on through the forest, my brain began to play a movie, memories from my first-ever job. I'd been a dishwasher at a little lake-side cafe in San Diego and there was a regular customer who'd come in almost every day to drink. He had advanced cancer, and large grapefruit-shaped tumors shown visibly through his clothing. My manager said he'd given up on the expensive cancer treatments, preferring instead to enjoy his final years in his own way. Drinking with his friends and telling stories at the bar.

I'd never understood the decision to discontinue treatment. If there was even a sliver of hope, wouldn't you want to try? But in some small way, this brief moment with the butterfly helped me to understand.

Yes, there is a time for treatment and doing all you can to hold on. I'm not saying give up without a fight. But there is also a time when there's nothing left to do. The moment where it's ok to say, "That's enough. Let me just set here and do this my way."

Chapter 57

The Power of Choice

Blueberry Lavender Lemonade, Cantaloupe Mint, Champagne Mango, Cucumber Jalapeño, Guava Peach, Hibiscus Starfruit, and dozens more! This place was everything a gourmet popsicle shop should be. I perused the long glass top freezer waiting for a flavor to catch my eye, but ultimately, I decided on something simple. I wasn't just there for dessert. I was on a mission.

The woman behind the counter looked at me and asked, "Did you decide on one?"

"Yes ma'am, one Pina Colada and one Peanut Butter Banana please"

She dutifully grabbed the two bars and rang me up, "That'll be $10.83."

I slid her a $10 and two $1's "Keep the change."

"Thanks," she says. "Have a nice day."

"You too."

I think it will be.

Picking up the two popsicles I exited the shop and started walking. A few stores away I saw a homeless man. He didn't ask me for anything when I passed him on my way in. He'd just sat there quietly holding out a cup, head hanging low.

As I approached, he held that same posture, an aura of defeat radiating from him.

In a conversational tone, I asked, "Hey man, can you help me with something?"

He raised his head to look at me for the first time. Then with a slight furrow in his brow he said, "Maybe?"

I pointed toward the popsicle shop and asked, "Have you ever been in that popsicle shop?"

He shook his head side to side defensively and said, "No, I ain't never been in there. Did they say something?"

"No, no. Nothing like that," I said. "It's just that I was in there a minute ago, and I bought these two popsicles." As I said it, I held them up in front of me.

He evaluated them for a moment, looking from one hand to the other, then looked back at me quizzically.

"I wasn't sure which one you'd prefer," I said, "so I got us a Peanut Butter Banana," emphasizing the one on my left hand, "and a Pina Colada," lifting my right.

With a noncommittal reply he said, "Oh. Uhhhh, either one."

"But which one would you prefer?" I asked.

He paused for a moment, and the slightest hint of a smile began to break the edges of his weather-beaten lips, but then it retreated. "Uhhhh, I don't know. You choose," he said.

Reassuringly I said, "I'm going to be very happy with either one. I'd like for you to pick."

This went back and forth a few more times. He was adamant about not choosing, but I stood firm, my price was his choice.

Finally, he realized I wasn't going to budge. He took one more look at each popsicle, then his eyes locked on one of my hands. I knew what he'd decided before he even spoke and whispered the words in unison with him, "Pina Colada." The tension between us instantly dissolved and a real smile spread across his face.

I extended my hand.

He accepted the popsicle.

"Thank you," he said simply.

"Pleasure," I replied. "You take care."

"You too," he said genuinely.

I turned and continued down the street.

* * *

This moment took me back to a summer when I was a child. I'd asked my parents for a toy train set. But they refused to buy it for me. Instead, they offered to give me opportunities to earn the money myself. They said it would teach me discipline and responsibility. I was only seven years old, so I didn't care much about that stuff, but I wanted a train set. So, I agreed and started working. I mowed the lawn, did extra chores, and helped with the family business. Once I'd earned $20, my mom took me to Bank of America to open a savings account. I had to stand in front of a scary man in a suit and answer questions I didn't totally understand. But after we were done, he handed me a little navy-blue booklet with a handwritten note inside that said, "Deposit, $20."

I still have that savings account today, 39 years later. And whether my childhood self enjoyed the process or not, I eventually earned enough to buy that train set. An experience that taught me discipline and responsibility.

I had no objective when I first approached this homeless man. My heart was moved by a man too broken to even ask for help. But as we began to speak, I noticed how he habitually avoided making choices. A habit that very likely contributed to his downtrodden state of affairs. That's why I dug my heels in. Happy as I was to give him an ice cream, he had to choose. Just as I'd had to choose whether I wanted to work for that train set or not. And because I refused to pardon him of that responsibility, he finally acquiesced. He made a choice.

It's easy to forget how empowered we are by the choices we make every day. You probably choose your clothing, car, location of residence, and cell phone provider, likely thinking nothing of it. But imagine if those choices were denied you? How might you feel? Or, worse yet, what if the thing you wrestled with most in life was the ability to choose? How paralyzing might it be if you couldn't bring yourself to make any choices? How would the winds and waves carry you to and fro without your say so?

I hope that in that moment of choice, this man found some empowerment. I hope it set off a domino run of choices in his life, a chain reaction that moved him towards some greater peace or comfort.

Chapter 58

Roadside Diner

S he stood behind the counter at this tired roadside diner. The delicate hint of a tear welling in her eye. Her lips quivered in time to the tune of the Adele song playing in the background. Stoically she wrapped silverware in napkins as the white bearded truck driver nearby sipped his coffee. He didn't notice the distress she was barely holding back. Sitting at my table, I wondered about her story. The song changed, and her frown lessened. The public face she wore that said, "Everything's okay," returned. I looked at the wall next to me. There was a series of scrapbooked picture frames, the kind that held seven to eight photos each. One read, "Live fully, cherish every moment." Around it, the pictures depicted a young man. He was smiling, hanging with friends, at a wedding in one, and fishing in another. Then as I looked closer, I saw that there was also a young woman in many of the images. She looked familiar, like a younger version of the waitress behind the counter. Now I realized this little restaurant was a daily reminder of the life they'd hoped to live together but never got to. And despite the years, her pain was fresh, a burden born daily. The mourning over that which could never be recovered.

So many times in life I've read some famous quote and thought, "That's good."

Then, a decade later, I come across that same quote and think, "Wow, that's profound."

Throw on ten more years and I see that quote again, but this time it hits differently. This time I've finally lived enough, and seen enough, and felt enough to actually understand what the author really meant.

When I saw this woman in the diner, I finally understood this one, "Everyone has their own struggles, regardless of whether you can see it or not."

For once, I could see it, like a billboard on her brow. And no one else could, even though it was right there, plain as day. Since then, I've tried to be even more understanding of others, because some are carrying a terrible invisible weight.

Chapter 59

The Lowly Handyman

She stops by the small room to check on my progress, "How's it coming?"

"It's good," I answer from my knelt position, "Almost done."

She points the wet paintbrush she's holding at me and says, "You are a lifesaver."

She begins to turn away but stops when I ask, "What are you painting out there?"

"Oh, we are re-creating Leonardo da Vinci's woman with an ermine." Her tone indicates it is a pursuit I'd have no interest in.

"Marvelous," I reply, "He is one of my favorite artists."

"Really? I would not have guessed you a fan of art." Her voice is skeptical.

"Have you ever been to the Hermitage Museum in St. Petersburg Russia?" I ask.

Her eyes widen, then fade with a faraway dreaminess, "No. But I've always wanted to go."

"Did you know that if you looked at every piece of art in the Hermitage for 10 seconds it would take seven years to see it all?"

"Goodness, I had no idea. Have you been there?"

I nod in the affirmative while I simultaneously manipulate a socket wrench, its mechanism clicks unobtrusively amidst our exchange.

"Wow, I hope to do that someday." she says, "I remember when I was in Florence, I went to see the David but the museum was closed, I was devastated."

"Oh no, you have to go back, the David is the most perfect work ever created by human hand."

"You've seen it as well?"

"Yes, and the Leonardo da Vinci Museum which is right down the street from it. Florence is one of my favorite cities."

"Wow, I never would've imagined."

"Don't worry," I say, "You will go back, you will see it."

She nods her head, and a small smile lifts her wrinkled cheeks. "I hope so."

Turning back to the toilet I've been fixing as we talked, I say "All right, that should do it. Your total will be $250 and we are all square."

Snapping back to the business at hand she says, "Of course, can I write you a check?"

Though handy, I didn't start life as a handyman. Handyman'ing was something I fell into while recovering from injuries that took me off the path of being a professional entertainer. But this little old lady didn't know anything about my past. She called me because a friend of hers had given a recommendation, and, because her toilet wasn't working. She couldn't have known that my younger self had dared to follow a dream that took me to 84 countries and every state in the US. An unlikely path considering my middle-class blue-collar upbringing. I very well could have become a career handyman instead of a late blooming one. But I'd lucked out, and had a glorious career full of experiences and places just like the ones we'd just discussed.

But that is secondary to the lesson I learned that day.

When she looked down at the scruffy man tightening the bolts on her toilet, she never imagined he'd share her interest in art. And maybe on the scale of probabilities her presumption had an edge over the alternative. But old and tired as it might be to say "Don't judge a book by its cover," we must continue to say it until the lesson is learned.

A life goes through many evolutions, and many chapters, so regardless of the uniform or suit or even dirty rags that you see on a person's back, you can never guess the depths of their being by sight alone. We must peel back the layers and go deeper, if we ever hope to truly understand one another.

Chapter 60

While Pumping Gas

I pulled into the station and got out to pump my gas, but before I even put my credit card in, a reasonably well-dressed guy walked up and started a conversation with me. I couldn't make out his motive right away, but his angle felt like a pitch, so I wasn't surprised when he finally asked for money. I told him I'd like to help, but things were tight that month. He was understanding and kept up the conversation with me for a few more minutes before excusing himself. Once he'd wandered away, I tried the card reader only to discover it was out of order. The black and grey digital display flashed, "see cashier." Well, this was one of my pet peeves at gas stations. I believe that a business should make it as easy as possible for you to spend your money, and unless I'm desperately low on fuel, I never "see the cashier." I just leave. And that's what I did, because catty corner to the gas station I'd just pulled into was another gas station. So, I got in my truck and drove across the street to the first available pump they had, then got out to fill my tank. As I did this, I saw that the man who'd just asked me for money was making his way across the street to the gas station I had just relocated to. As he walked up, I nodded at him in recognition, but he started into the exact same pitch he'd hit me with on the other side of the street. Of course, this was surprising, but I decided to play along and see what would happen. He asked me where I was originally from, a question he'd just asked me moments before. I told him again, "San Diego." When I said that I could see a flash of remembrance in his eyes, but he still couldn't place me. Hesitating a little he asked, "Wait a minute, do I know you?"

With a friendly smile I said, "We've met once before."

Feigning recognition he asked, "Are you staying at the motel around the corner?"

"No, no. We actually met right over there," I said pointing across the street.

He turned and looked in the hopes it would jog his memory, and sure enough it did. Turning back he said, "Wait, weren't you just over there?"

"Yes sir," I answered nodding my head. "The machine wouldn't take my card, so I pulled in over here."

His eyes widened as if he'd just witnessed a supernatural event.

"Man, you really had me going. I knew you looked familiar!"

"Well, it was good chatting with you, again," I said.

"Yeah, yeah, I better get going," he answered as he turned to move along.

The reason this really stood out to me is that when he'd first approached me, we'd had a pretty legitimate and friendly conversation. He really made it feel like an afterthought that he was asking for money, rather than the primary motivation for him talking to me. But then he saw me 90 seconds later and had no recollection whatsoever. I realized I wasn't a real person to him. I was a handout. I either had something to give, or I didn't.

Sometimes I wonder if the homeless and/or addicted amongst us are examples of humanity in its rawest form. Displaying only the loosest of civility and pretense to mask their actual desires. Whereas the higher one climbs in society, the more complex and difficult it becomes to decipher what someone's actual motivations are. As those masks grow in complexity, the depth and breadth of the schemes grow along with them. In a way, the simplicity of an exchange with the homeless is refreshing. Almost without exception, I know what they want.

Chapter 61

Forever Person

This morning as I walked along the beach, I saw a man and woman together. She is in speed walker gear, tennis shoes, short runner's shorts and a long sleeve hoodie to ward off the cold. Next to her walked a man, who in comparison looked unsteady. One of his legs drug slightly, leaving irregular footprints in the sand. His left arm was permanently bent 90° at the elbow, likely the result of a stroke or some neurological affliction. They have the air of two people who've spent many years together. That calm familiarity that radiates connection even when there's no physical contact or words exchanged. Seeing them together exercising, her going a little slower than she could comfortably go, while he went a little faster than his failing body might have preferred, I could tell they were still matching each other step for step.

Whenever I see people together, especially when one of them has slipped from the splendor they likely had in the relationship's early years, I believe in humanity again.

So often people say that they are looking for their forever person. But I've come to realize that phrase doesn't really mean anything. The only way you'll ever know if the person next to you is your forever person is if one day far in the future, you're lying in your hospital bed and right there beside you is that person; still there, holding your hand.

The day you think to yourself, "Whether I'm the one in the hospital bed looking at them, or the one sitting next to the bed holding their hand, I'll be there."

That's the day you know you're with your forever person.

Because the secret to finding your forever person has little to do with anyone else. It's something you cultivate within yourself. It's about becoming a forever person.

How can we expect someone else to give us this thing if we aren't willing to give it to them?

Maybe if we all stop trying to find that forever person and start working on becoming a forever person instead, soon we'd all be enjoying a little more support and connection.

Chapter 62

Step Into it

Wringing out the hot soapy rag I continued scrubbing the wire rack. Once it was clean I would be able to organize all my books and office supplies. Out of nowhere Lulu, my black and white tuxedo kitty jumped onto the shelf with a loud, "Meow!"

I jumped, partly startled, partly playing along. She likes to surprise me. Taking two more steps, she walked right into the area I was trying to clean and stood there defiantly. Playfully I chastise her, "What are *you* doing?!?"

She turned in a circle playfully, "Meow! Meeeeow!" she exclaimed.

"I'm almost done," I told her. Then gently poking her back leg I said, "Move, shoo!"

With each of my pokes, she meowed grouchily, then hurried to one side of the rack and prepared to jump down. I watched as she spotted her landing, firmed her feet, and then launched toward the floor. But as her front feet left the shelf, one of her back legs lost its grip on the thin wire and fell through one of the openings. Instantly I realized what was about to happen.

Imagine yourself jumping off the top of a six-foot tall fence, but having all your weight stopped because your leg is trapped between two steel bars. And the frontmost bar is racked against your shin catching *all* of your weight. It would be excruciatingly painful!

That's what Lulu was about to experience. Everything went into slow motion, and my brain presented two options:

1. I can't get to her fast enough to stop it, but if I grab her now, I'll be able to reduce the amount of time she'll be hung up. However, I'm also going to be grabbing her right when the pain starts. I know she'll panic and think I'm attacking her. Naturally, she's going to claw and bite the heck out of me because she won't understand that I'm trying to help.

Or, 2. Let it happen, wait to see if she works herself loose, and hope she doesn't break her leg in the process.

The choice was easy. I reached for her immediately. I saw the leg wedge, her body folded on itself before stopping abruptly, her momentum halted entirely by her shin bone.

The yowl that came out of her was two-toned. It began with a typical, *"Yeowl"* of pain, but instantly evolved into a panicked screech. I grabbed her and felt the fur already standing on end. Quickly I lifted to relieve the pressure on the leg. But she was in buzzsaw mode. Claws and teeth tore my flesh, both hands, both arms. Like sinking your hands into a running blender.

As soon as her leg was free, I let go. She landed on her feet and shot out of the room like a bullet. I watched her departure to see if the back leg appeared damaged, but it looked okay.

Glancing down at my hands, I assessed the damage. Blood dripped freely from the 12 or so gashes in my fingers. The punctures in my right hand where she'd bitten hadn't yet started to bleed but promised to deliver soon. The long shallower streaks on my forearms lazily leaked plasma. All in all, it wasn't bad, nothing that wouldn't heal in a week or two.

I walked to the kitchen sink to wash, then grabbed a handful of paper towels and applied pressure to my fingers to stop the bleeding.

Thinking back over what happened, I had no regrets. If I had to do it ten more times, I'd handle it the exact same way every time.

Helping my cat wasn't a life-threatening situation; it was just a few scratches. But it's a small reminder that sometimes in life you'll be called to, "Step into it." In those moments, you may be tempted to preserve yourself, avoid injury, or choose to not get involved. That's natural. Our impulse for self-preservation is imperative to our survival. And you should always do all that you can to ensure that you come home safely to your family and loved ones. They depend on you, and they need you. That said, a man must protect their loved ones at all costs. It's not a pleasant thing to consider, but one day you may need to overpower your self-preservation reflex in order to do something that needs to be done.

If that moment ever comes do not be afraid. Take a deep breath, then step into it.

Chapter 63

Black Cat

As I pulled into my driveway after a late night gig, I saw a stray kitty that had been hit by a car. I went to check on him and saw from the unnatural alignment of his spine that the collision had been fatal. But other than that, he was entirely intact. I considered the options for a few moments. Who could I call at 2 am? I had to be up early the next day. What if he was someone's pet? As I stared down at him, looking so peaceful in the moonlight, I decided it couldn't wait until morning. Walking towards the backyard I collected a shovel, lighter, and two latex gloves. Then setting my phone to play on repeat, I selected, "Bright Eyes" by Art Garfunkel. Lighting two oil lamps so I'd have some light to work by, I started digging a hole between our mango and mulberry trees. After I'd prepared a nice place for him, making sure it was deep enough, wide enough and smooth across the bottom, I returned to the front yard. Putting on the latex gloves, I knelt next to him and gently caressed his head. His ears did not fold back the way a cat's ears normally do, but rather stayed perked, popping back into position after each caress. I whispered, "What a sweet, beautiful boy you are. I wish I could have known you before all this." Gently, I lifted him and carried him to the backyard. When I got there, the song "Bright Eyes" had just begun to play anew, so I set him next to the hole and gave him soft loving pets. I told him about our place, about the different trees, and that our chicken Snowflake was buried only a few feet away to keep him company. He didn't move or change a thing, but he seemed more at peace laying on natural earth than he had out on the asphalt. Soon the song came to an end, and placing my hand on his neck reassuringly I asked, "Are you ready?" The light from the torch flickered in the night breeze, casting undulating shadows across his jet-black fur. It created a feeling of acceptance, so I lifted him one last time to place him into the earth. As I did, a small cave in at the edge of the hole deposited a dusting of dirt on his left cheek. As the song played on, I cleaned the dirt away. Even though I knew I was going to cover him up in a few moments, that will be intentional dirt. Then, before filling it in, I took one last moment to say farewell.

Rest well beautiful boy.

In life, there will be things that are clearly your responsibility. And there will be things that are clearly someone else's responsibility. But for everything else, everything that doesn't seem to fall neatly into anyone's realm of responsibility, those things are special. Those things are everyone's responsibility. Yours and mine, to handle as stewards of the earth.

* * *

Recently, a kid who rides his bike up and down our street stopped over to see what we were doing in the garden. I quickly put him to work, though, at eight years old, Hector's help is often more play than it is help.

After a while, I noticed that a squirrel had been hit by a car in front of our house. I asked Hector to grab a shovel, and he bounded off to get one. When he returned, he asked, "What we doin' now?"

"Man stuff," I responded. "You feeling up for some man stuff?"

His eight-year-old eyes fretted in thought, then, with a feigned bravado he said, "Ok."

"Alright, let's go."

We looked both ways to make sure it was clear, then we walked out to the squirrel. Getting closer I saw that all his insides had become outsides. It sure wasn't pretty. Holding out the shovel I asked Hector, "You wanna scoop him up?"

"What! Why?" Hector exclaimed.

"We need to bury him," I said.

Hector's forehead furrowed again, then he slowly reached out to take the shovel.

"Ok, one swift scoop now, try to get him in one go."

Hector lined up on the squirrel, focusing like a fighter pilot in a training simulation. Then he slid the shovel forward, neatly scooping the vast majority in one go.

With a look of triumph he asked, "Now what?"

"Now we need to bury him," I answered leading him back towards the yard.

He dutifully followed, and once there, we dug a hole next to the bananas for the squirrel.

After all was done, I asked Hector, "How do you feel?"

"Sad," he said.

"Yeah, that's ok. It was sad," I said.

"Why'd we do that?" he asked.

"Because it needed to be done," I said, "And if we hadn't done it who would have?" I asked.

Hector thought long and hard about whose job it was to take care of these kinds of things. Then, shrugging his shoulders he said, "I dunno?"

"Exactly," I said, "Anytime you can't think whose responsibility something is, ask if maybe it isn't something you can take care of yourself. And if it is, just take care of it, like we did with this squirrel. That's part of what being a man is all about, taking care of the things nobody else wants to take care of. Not necessarily because we even want to, but because we can. Understand?"

"Yeah," he said, "But I'm still sad."

"It's ok to be sad. I get sad too sometimes."

Perking in excitement Hector asked, "Can I decorate the grave?"

"Absolutely! But if you're going to cut any of the garden flowers make sure you ask Miss Stephanie first, ok?"

"Okay," he said, already running towards a nearby flowerbed.

I remember so much from when I was eight years old, I wonder how much he'll remember when he's my age. Will he one day teach a neighbor kid how to bury a squirrel, too? I hope so.

Chapter 64

Wanna Bet

I pulled my truck into Home Depot, found a good parking spot, and prepared to head in when I spied a man in dirty mismatched clothes wandering between the store entrance and exit doors. Pointing towards the homeless man I asked my friend, "Hey, do you think he'll ask us for money on our way in, or do you think he'll wait until we're coming out of the store to ask?"

Noticing the man for the first time, my buddy said, "Man, he's not gonna ask us for anything."

Looking at him seriously I said, "What do you wanna bet?"

Knowing I'm not the betting type, and realizing I'm actually going somewhere with this, my friend took another look at the man. I watched as he weighed the options, then, seemingly satisfied with his original answer he said, "Yeah, he's spaced out. I don't think he'll ask us for anything."

Looking at him confidently I said, "Okay, if you're right and he doesn't ask us for money at all, I'll buy you lunch for a week. Or, if he asks us for money on our way into the store, I'll *still* buy you lunch for a week! *But*, if he asks us for money on our way out, you have to buy me lunch today. How does that sound?"

Looking at me with wide eyes, then breaking into a loud confident laugh he said, "It sounds like you're going to be buying me some lunches!"

Both laughing now, we shook hands on it. Then I said, "Ok, let's go."

As we walked across the parking lot, the homeless man paid no attention to us at all, allowing us to walk into the store unchallenged.

As soon as we were inside and out of earshot shot my friend confidently said, "See, I told you. That guy is out of it. He didn't even see us!"

"We'll see," I answer.

After gathering our items and heading to check out, we walked through the exit door. Sure enough, the homeless man was still there, and as we passed by, he ignored us completely. With each step I felt my buddy's excitement rise. He thought he won, but I knew what was coming. I could feel it in my bones.

We took a few more steps before a soft raspy voice found our ears, "Spare some change fellas?"

Out of the corner of my eye I saw my friend's jaw drop. He couldn't believe it. I turned back and looked at the man, "Sorry bud, I'm not carrying any cash."

Then my friend turned back to the guy and said, "Yeah, I got a couple of bucks." Then with a sidelong glance in my direction retorted, "Since I'm already buying your tall ass lunch anyway, what's an extra couple bucks!"

He walked back to hand over the cash while I continued on to the truck. I heard them chatting a little as the money was exchanged.

A minute later my buddy caught up and climbed into the cab of the truck. As soon as his door shut, he started shouting, "*Omg*, how did you know that?"

"Easy," I answer, "The guy understands human nature."

"Nature sccchhhhmature," my friend scoffs, "I'm asking, *how* did you *know that*? That was some Batman shit right there!"

Probably sounding a little too much like a college professor I said,

"When a person is walking into a store, they're on a mission. They have an objective. They're thinking about all the things they need to get, how much it's going to cost, etc. The last thing they want is to be interrupted. And they're definitely not going to hand out their hard-earned money to someone only to walk in the store moments later and spend even more. Furthermore, when a person is walking up to a store and they see a homeless person, they instinctively brace. They're expecting to be hit up for money. They are already preparing to say no. So, it's a terrible time to ask someone for money. And through experience, the homeless guy has learned this. So instead, he waits. He lets himself be seen by the person as they walk into the store, and instead of asking for anything, he ignores them, which is a subtle guilt trip. Because the person who was already preparing to say no ends up passing by without any interruption at all, and internally they feel bad. They feel bad for having judged him, for having assumed he would ask.

Now their guard is lowered. They do their shopping, accomplish their tasks, spend their money, and walk out the door. By now they've almost forgotten about the homeless guy, but then they see him again and that familiar resistance rises up inside them. But then they remember that he didn't ask for anything before, and how bad they'd felt. So, their guard stays low as they try to think the best of him. And true to form, once again, he allows them to pass by unmolested, not asking for a thing. Now their defenses drop completely. The threat has passed, and there's no reason to be on guard anymore. They sigh a relaxed sigh because it confirms what they'd already thought; they were judging and being unfair. But then, gently, almost as an afterthought, the guy softly asks for some change. Now their generous side overpowers all reason. The homeless man has built trust simply by being unobtrusive, and suddenly they feel their hands searching for a handful of change or a few dollars to give. It's brilliant."

My friend looked at me with an expression I couldn't quite read. Then he said, "Wow, where did you read that?"

"I didn't," I answered, "I've just been watching and slowly building it as a hypothesis over the years."

Shaking his head slightly a smile cracked his face, "Man, don't you have anything better to think about? You really should do something with that big brain of yours."

We both laugh at this, then pull out of the parking spot, drive out to the street, and stop at the red light on the corner. That's when we realized that we had forgotten one of the most important items that we needed to get at Home Depot. Lifting our hands in frustration, I made a right on red and returned to the parking lot. We even parked in the same spot since it was still open, and the homeless man was still there.

With a feigned seriousness my friend looked at me and said, "Hey, you see that guy, what do you wanna bet he doesn't ask us for money?"

"Why wouldn't he ask us for money?" I asked.

Throwing his hands in the air like I'm an idiot my friend shouted, "Because I just gave him money! Duh!"

With a serious look on my face I said, "You wanna go double or nothing?"

"Double or nothing," he asked. "What are you talking about?"

"Double or nothing, same deal as before, two weeks of lunches if I'm wrong; you buy lunch today and tomorrow if I'm right," I offered.

"What, that he'll ask me for money on the way out?" he asked, clearly perplexed.

"More than that," I said. "Not only will he ask you for money on the way out just like before, he also won't remember you *at all*."

Looking like he just won the lottery my friend screams, "*Duuuu-uude*, I'm about to smoke you! What do you *mean* he won't remember me, I just gave him money *and* talked to him!"

Still looking at him with a totally serious face, "Exactly. That's my offer, double or nothing. What do you say?"

Hesitating slightly because of my confidence, he looked at the guy through the window for a few seconds. "Man, okay, you're on!"

We shook again and he walked back into the store to grab our missing item.

As predicted, the man ignored him completely on the way in.

Then five or ten minutes later, when I saw my friend emerge from the exit doors, the man once again allowed him to pass without a word. From where I was parked, my friend and I could hold eye contact, and even though I couldn't hear it, I saw the moment the man asked for money. My friend stopped in his tracks right there, holding eye contact with me. He shook his head in disbelief, then he turned back and started chatting with the guy. Maybe 30 seconds passed before my friend broke off the interaction and came back to the truck. The look on his face said it all. Opening the door and getting in he sat quietly for a moment, refusing to break the silence or make eye contact.

Finally, I said, "Well, what happened?"

He burst out, "Just shut up and drive to Chick-Fil-A so I can buy you lunch Rainman!" Then shaking his head again, he gave me a sidelong glance that spoke volumes.

Chapter 65

The Honey Bee

While pulling weeds in the garden I noticed a honeybee dutifully flying from tiny flower to tiny flower. He was methodical, landing to conserve energy when it was beneficial, taking off, landing again, and so on. Then I noticed that the flowers he was investigating were fantastically small. Maybe even suspiciously small. So, I looked closer, and only then did I realize that the bee was not gathering nectar from tiny flowers. Instead, he was investigating the dozens of tiny spots that had fallen onto the leaves a few days earlier while I was cleaning white paint out of a brush. To his eyes the droplets looked just like tiny flowers, and though he visited each, none of them yielded the prize he sought.

I felt bad that my carelessness while cleaning the brush had caused this creature unnecessary effort. I never imagined a thing as small as paint splatters could have an effect on the world.

Chapter 66

Humans and Nothing More

The white cloud looked like harmless steam until I breathed it in. Then the acrid vapor burned my lungs and throat. The smell of battery acid smoldering on a hot engine is something you never forget. Continuing past the vapor I saw a large white SUV. Its front end was smashed so severely that part of the headlight harness was touching the base of the shattered windshield. The driver was in place but was sitting so far back it looked like his seat was reclined. Moving closer I saw the dashboard of the vehicle had taken over the area where he would normally sit, pushing him back and pinning him in the process. The driver's side window was blown out, so I leaned in and shouted, "Are you ok?"

As if nothing at all were out of the ordinary, he casually answered, "Yeah, just help me push this off'a me."

A blood-curdling scream comes from the passenger seat, "Help my boyfriend!"

Looking over I saw his girlfriend was still in her seat, and through her passenger side window, I saw two people running up to help her. I turned my attention back to the driver. I realized there was no way I would be able to get him out. The steering wheel was nowhere to be seen, and the side door was crushed in over the top of him. I couldn't even make out what half of the dashboard components used to be because they were so mangled. But he was remarkably stable all considered, breathing didn't seem restricted, and the bloody gashes on his arm didn't require immediate care. I got his attention and said, "Help is coming. I'll be right back."

He nodded distractedly, still trying to figure out how to push the dashboard off with the one unpinned arm he had available.

Turning to the right I ran to the second vehicle, a white minivan that looked like something out of a war movie. Its side door was either camouflaged against the wreckage or missing entirely, which left a wide opening for me to enter. Stepping in I looked for injured passengers, but quickly realized it was empty.

Exiting the van I looked back towards the SUV where the guy was pinned. From this angle, the car looked like a slain beast bleeding out every imaginable fluid in its death throes. Dark puddles fanned out steadily across the asphalt. The realization that a vehicle fire could kick off at any second hit me. And without any way to free the driver, it would be catastrophic.

Just then a dark luxury car pulled up and a short, slightly over-weight man got out.

"Do you have a fire extinguisher?" I yelled to him.

"No," he answered calmly as he walked towards the SUV.

"Ok, call 911 then," I shouted as I jogged towards the SUV.

Stopping to look at me the man smiled and said, "I'm an off-duty police officer. You call 911!"

"Yes sir," I answered, reaching for my phone. Knowing he was there took some of the pressure off. I could take charge in high-stakes scenarios when needed, but it wasn't my job. This was what he was trained for, so I was happy to adopt a support role.

Almost immediately an operator picked up with a professional tone, "911, what's your emergency?"

As I described the scene to her and answered questions, the off-duty officer went over and tried to pull open the driver-side door where the man was trapped, but it wouldn't budge. Several other good Samaritans grabbed on and tried to help, but even working together it was too strong for them.

Moments later a man I hadn't seen before ran into the area between the wrecked vehicles and started clearing people out. Then he turned and motioned to a brand-new white jeep sitting just outside the ring of chaos. The driver of the jeep pulled in hesitantly, and I'm completely baffled by what they're doing until the man ran over and grabbed the winch cable attached to her front bumper. He pulled hard but it won't move, so he shouted for the Jeep driver to release the cable. She looked down at the controls helplessly then yelled back, "I don't know how. I've never used it before!" Running over and opening her door, he quickly found the controls and showed her how to unlock it. Then he and the off-duty officer drug the cable towards the SUV where they wrapped it around the driver's door. But before they could activate the winch, an on-duty police officer arrived and stopped them. The man who'd had the idea of using the winch in the first place started to argue with her, but the roar of nearby fire trucks cut him off. Professional help was arriving, so it was better to let them handle it.

I ended the 911 call and looked around at the small army of good Samaritans who had descended upon the scene.

On the other side of the SUV, I saw the man's girlfriend. She was still with the two people who'd originally come to her window. They were comforting her as best they could.

The lady officer was with the man trapped in the vehicle. I couldn't hear what she was saying but based on his expression, it was the right thing because he was waiting calmly.

The man who'd waved over the lady in the jeep was helping get the winch wound up and stowed so she could get her vehicle out of the way of the incoming firetrucks.

And the off-duty police officer walked over to me and said, "You might want to move your vehicle because once the fire trucks are here, you'll be boxed in."

"Yes sir," I answered, quickly moving to get my car out of the way.

As I started to get in the vehicle, the off-duty officer looked back at me once more and with a nod yelled, "Hey, keep it up!"

"You too," I yelled back, grateful to have been acknowledged as a concerned citizen rather than getting yelled at or told I was in the way.

Jumping into the car I rolled out moments before a big firetruck pulled into the spot where I'd just been parked.

I don't know how things turned out after I left. I never heard another thing about it. But that's not the reason I wanted to share this story. The real reason is the handful of details I deliberately left out in the telling, the details that I believe make the story special.

Because I will never forget the night a black man and his black girlfriend had a terrible car accident. I won't forget the two white women who ran up and comforted her. Or the female highway patrol officer who stayed with the trapped man. I won't forget the portly Hispanic off-duty police officer who told me to call 911. Or the middle eastern man in a full turban, who helped the well-dressed Hispanic lady in the jeep unwind her winch. None of those things mattered in that moment. No one cared about differences in belief or culture or gender. For just a little while we were humans and nothing more.

The End

Thank you for purchasing and reading my book. I am grateful and hope you found value in reading it. Please consider sharing it with friends or family and leaving a review online. Your support allows me to continue down the path of creation. Always, Bill Berry

Chapter 67

Coming Soon

Book two, as yet untitled, will cover the first seven years of my journey towards becoming a professional entertainer. How I left school, had corrective heart surgery, and ended up working four different part time jobs only to quit them all to chase a dream. It was hard, it was uncertain, and it was the best decision I ever made.

I also plan to include helpful tips for anyone chasing dreams of their own. No two journeys are ever the same, but there is value in exchanging notes.

As you've joined me here, I hope you'll join me again when it's ready.

- The First Gig -

The hotel clerk barely noticed me, but the family waiting in line stared openly. I couldn't blame them. My black boots with 2-inch lifts made my normal 6'5" stature even more imposing. I stood steady, shoulders back, dark cape blowing in the breeze made by the fan above the hotel's automatic doors. Pulling back the cuff of my over-sized black leather glove I tried to make out the time. The mask I was wearing had lenses darker than welding goggles, but if I held the watch right in front of my eyes, I could see it. 5:37 pm. I was late. Well, kinda. I had arrived over an hour ago, but the banquet hall where the performance was supposed to be happening was empty. I wondered if they had rescheduled and forgot to tell the booking agent. It would be a bummer if it was canceled, but also, it wouldn't. This was my first gig, and though on the outside I looked like a supervillain, on the inside, I was petrified. Not knowing what else to do, I waited, secretly hoping it was canceled so I could go home. Taking a seat in one of the lobby chairs, I contemplated how I got here. The spotlight was the sworn enemy of all introverts, so in high school I'd steered clear of the limelight. I preferred the backstage theater environment that involved building sets, flying scenery, running shows, etc. I never imagined that one day I'd be the one *on* the stage. But here I was.

The thick costume blanketed me from head to toe and I was sweating despite the AC. I considered taking off the helmet, but the booking agent's words echoed in my mind, "Once you are in charac-ter, stay in character. Don't ever let them see you half in and half out of costume. It destroys the illusion."

Suddenly, an overly done up woman with long bleached blonde hair stormed into the lobby.

"Oh my god" she screams, "We've been looking *everywhere* for you! Come on, you're late!"

Without waiting she spun on her red 3″ heels and darted back out to the parking lot.

I ran after her, surprised by her speed. When I caught up, I started to apologize but it died on my lips. Her expression was pure disgust.

A few more steps and we entered a building almost identical to the one I'd just been waiting in. That's when I realized what had happened. Though I was at the right hotel, I was in the wrong building.

A long, red carpet led to a set of double doors. To each side was a stormtrooper. Their pearly white armor gleamed in sharp contrast to the black laser blasters they carried.

Grabbing me by the shoulders the blonde turned me towards her. With a trained eye she quickly adjusted my cape, fixed a cuff, and straightened my plastic breastplate. Finally satisfied, her Botox-infused cheeks cracked under a forced smile that revealed unnaturally white teeth. In a voice that dripped honey she said, "Time for your big entrance."

On cue the Star Wars theme music, "Imperial March" began. The double doors burst open and the two stormtroopers charged inside. Fog machines belched smoke from behind large plastic palm trees to augment our entrance. Stepping into the darkened room I could feel the music as it buffeted me. The swirling party lights created a visual kaleidoscope in the helmet. I couldn't see but continued forward, hoping not to run into someone or trip over something.

I heard the DJ over the mic, "Uhhh ohhh, it's Darrrrrth Vaderrrr!"

The crowd roared and clapped.

The DJ continued, "Who will save us from this terrible evil?"

The crowd cheered again, then they started chanting something I couldn't make out.

Low and to the right, a sliver of green light appeared. Dancing irregularly, the light grew larger and larger. An anticipatory hush fell over the crowd.

Suddenly the green light shot straight at my face. I raised my own lightsaber, but not fast enough. The green light changed into hard plastic as it slashed into the side of my head.

The crowd let out that sound they do when a boxer takes a punch.

I heard Velcro rip as the two halves of the helmet I was wearing tore apart. The face mask portion went one way, the helmet portion went the other, each clanking like cheap plastic as they tumbled across the dance floor.

My ears rang from the attack but now that the helmet was off, I could see. Beyond the dance floor was a bandstand where the DJ was set up. He was still holding the mic, but in his surprise, the words stopped flowing. To the left were the adult partygoers, several of whom had brought a hand up to cover their mouths the way people do when they feel powerless to do anything else. To my right are all the kids, mostly boys. They looked awkward in their tween-age bodies and un-tailored off the shelf dress clothes. In my peripheral vision I caught a hint of the green light. Turning towards it, I came face to face with my attacker, figuratively. He couldn't be an inch over five feet tall, but he stood like a warrior, legs wide, knees bent, chest heaving beneath the thin fabric of his short sleeved white button down. In his hands he held an extendable lightsaber, now broken by his attempt to behead me. It sagged like a jumbo green bendy straw. Our "battle" was over, and I was tempted to put a conciliatory hand on top of his head, but then stopped myself. Maybe there was some prohibition about touching someone else's yarmulke. Sensing everyone's eyes on me, I suddenly felt self-conscious. Earlier that day I had considered shaving, but then figured, "I'll be in a helmet, no one's going to see me anyway." Un-heroically I hurried over to where the face mask had landed and put it back on. Then holding it in place with one hand I half jogged to the other corner of the dance floor to grab the helmet portion. As I put it all back together, the booker's voice popped into my head again, "After the fight, make a big deal about how big and strong the kid is. Say that he is no longer a boy, that he is now a man and has proven himself." As if she heard the voice too, a random woman took my arm and walked me to the DJ stand. I passed behind the sound equipment, taking care not to trip on the cords and wires, before joining the DJ in his booth. He handed me a piece of paper and whispered, "They want you to read this." Then he turned to the crowd, lifted the mic to his mouth and said, "Darth Vader will now give a speech." I looked down at the handwritten message, but with the helmet on I couldn't make it out. I tried holding it right in front of my face, but there was still not enough light. Finally, I noticed that the DJ had a little lamp on his control panel. I placed the paper right under the bulb, but it was *still* too dark for me to see. An uncomfortable amount of time passed, and the crowd started to murmur. Sensing that the speech was not going to happen, the DJ announced, "Looks like Darth Vader can't read." Hearing this the crowd erupted into laughter, and by their laughter, I was truly vanquished. Stepping off the bandstand I made my way back across the dance floor. Smelling blood in the water one of the boys yelled out, "You're not the real Darth Vader!" Then as a group they started chanting, "You're not real, you're not real!" I wanted to be angry with them, but they were right; I wasn't real.

Without stopping to speak with the clients, pick up a check, or anything, I fled to my car. Finally safe in the front seat, the adrenaline wore off enough that I looked in the rear-view mirror to see if anyone was looking for me. Unsurprisingly, there was no entourage of fans lining up for my autograph. But spying my own reflection I realized that on the dance floor I hadn't put the helmet back on right. The face part looked good. It was hard to mess that up because your chin sits in the bottom of the mask. But the helmet part can Velcro on at a variety of angles, and in this case, I had placed it with a distinct forward tilt. The result was that Darth's forehead was almost completely covered, making the face seem unnaturally short and sunken above the eyes. I was sure everyone at the party was thinking it. I'd done my first ever gig looking like Darth Vader's Neanderthal ancestor. Humiliated, I started the car and drove out of the parking lot. I didn't even take the helmet off until I was several blocks away. I didn't want anyone to see me, remember me, or in any way think of this day ever again. My first gig went so poorly, I vowed to never perform again. And I believed it was the end of my journey as an entertainer. But life has a funny way of turning out differently than we expect...

About the Author

Guinness World Record holding sword swallower, three time world champion juggler, professional entertainer, yoga instructor, and author. Bill Berry has entertained on dozens of cruise ships, at 100's of colleges, countless corporate events, and 11 MWR military tours. With over 7,000 shows to his credit, he's visited 84 countries and every state in the US. And while he was doing all that, he wrote down the interesting things that happened along the way. Millions of words flowed from his fingers, and now he's ready to open the vault. With a focus on allegorical non-fiction and the moments in life that move, his style has been described as "Chicken Soup for the Soul" meets "The Endless Summer." He currently resides in Saint Petersburg, Florida, with his wife and two tuxedo kitties.

"Stories That Move" is Bill's first book.

Find me on social media: mrbillberry

www.ingramcontent.com/pod-product-compliance
Lightning Source LLC
Chambersburg PA
CBHW071154130626

46553CB00004B/1657